HODGE
LIBRARY - FT. MYERS

P9-CMY-561

WHAT I BELIEVE 2

Listening and Speaking about What Really Matters

MARY E. WARD

PEARSON
Longman

HODGES UNIVERSITY
LIBRARY, FT. MYERS

What I Believe 2

Copyright © 2008 by Pearson Education Inc.

All rights reserved.

No part of this publication may be reproduced, stored in a retrieval system, or transmitted in any form or by any means, electronic, mechanical, photocopying, recording, or otherwise, without the prior permission of the publisher.

Pearson Education, 10 Bank Street, White Plains, NY 10606

Staff credits: The people who made up the **What I Believe 2** team, representing editorial, production, design, and manufacturing, are Eleanor Barnes, John Beaumont, Elizabeth Carlson Nan Clarke, Stacey Hunter, Amy McCormick, Michael Mone, Rob Ruvo, Keyana Shaw, Debbie Sistino, Paula Van Ells, and Patricia Wosczyk.

Cover design: Patricia Wosczyk

Cover art: Quint Buchholz

Text design: Wanda España

Text composition: Laserwords

Audio and text credits: "Finding Prosperity by Feeding Monkeys," "In Praise of the 'Wobblies,'" "The Optimism of Jazz," "Always Go," "The Making of Poems," "When Ordinary People Achieve Extraordinary Things," "Disrupting My Comfort Zone," "A Goal of Service to Humankind," "Creative Solutions to Life's Challenges," "In Giving I Connect with Others," "A Balance Between Nature and Nurture" *All Copyright © 2008 by Pearson Education. Copyright © 2006 by This I Believe, Inc. Reprinted by permission of Henry Holt and Company, LLC.* "Free Minds and Hearts at Work" Copyright ©1951 by Jackie Robinson. Copyright © 2006 by This I Believe, Inc. Reprinted by permission of This I Believe, Inc. Gregory Orr, "Father's Song" from *The Caged Owl: New and Selected Poems.* Copyright © 2002 by Gregory Orr. Reprinted with the permission of Copper Canyon Press, www.coppercanyonpress.org

Photo credits: **Pages iv, 1** Nubar Alexanian, **p. 3** STR/AFP/Getty Images, **p. 7** Howard Davies/Corbis, **p. 11** Quint Buchholz, **pp. iv, 12** Time & Life Pictures/Getty Images, **p. 13** Stockbyte/Getty Images, **p. 18** Getty Images, **p. 22** Quint Buchholz, **pp. iv, 23** Nubar Alexanian, **p. 24** Katsutoshi Hatsuzawa/NEOVISION/Getty Images, **p. 28** Art Becker/Stone/Getty Images, **p. 33** Quint Buchholz, **pp. iv, 34** Nubar Alexanian, **p. 35** Owen Franken/Corbis, **p. 38** Rudi Von Briel/Photo Edit, **p. 43** Quint Buchholz, **pp. iv, 44** Nubar Alexanian, **p. 45** Beth Dixson/Alamy, **p. 49** David De Lossy/Getty Images, **p. 53** Quint Buchholz, **pp. iv, 54** Nubar Alexanian, **p. 55** Ed Darack/Getty Images, **p. 60** © 2007 International Campaign to Ban Landmines, **p. 65** Quint Buchholz, **pp. iv, 66** Nubar Alexanian, **p. 67** Tony Freeman/Photo Edit, **p. 70** MAPS.com/Corbis, **p. 76** Quint Buchholz, **pp. iv, 77** Nubar Alexanian, **p. 83** Noel Hendrickson/Getty Images, **p. 88** Quint Buchholz, **pp. iv, 89** Kevin Flores, **p. 90** Martin Harvey/Getty Images, **p. 92** Tom Grill/Corbis, **p. 94** Images.com/Corbis, **p. 98** Quint Buchholz, **pp. iv, 99** © 2008 The Associated Press, **p. 105** © 2008 The Associated Press, **p. 109** Quint Buchholz, **pp. iv, 110** Nubar Alexanian, **p. 112** Corbis, **p. 114** Courtesy Isabel Allende, **p. 119** Quint Buchholz, **pp. iv, 120** Nubar Alexanian, **p. 122** Photo Disc/Getty Images, **p. 126** Getty Images, **p. 131** Quint Buchholz.

Library of Congress Cataloging-in-Publication Data

Ward, Mary E.

What I believe 2 : listening and speaking about what really matters / Mary E. Ward.

p. cm.

ISBN 978-0-13-159193-6 (student book : alk. paper)

ISBN 978-0-13-159194-3 (audio)

ISBN 978-0-13-159196-7 (teacher's manual and answer key : alk. paper) 1. English language—Study and Teaching—Foreign speakers. 2. Communicative competence. I. Title. II. Title: What I believe two.

PE1128.A2W259 2008

428.2'4—dc22

2007048560

Printed in the United States of America

2 3 4 5 6 7 8 9 10—CRK—13 12 11 10 09 08

ACKNOWLEDGMENTS

Special thanks to my family: **Luca**, **Mark**, **Francesca**, and **Alda**; and to **Marion Burrows**, my high school English teacher; **John Beaumont**, for having faith in me; **Stacey Hunter**, for having patience and helping me see all sides of an idea; **Elizabeth Böttcher**, for her collaboration; and to the American Language Program, Columbia University.

—*Mary E. Ward*

Pearson Longman gratefully recognizes the cooperation of **Dan Gediman**, producer of *This I Believe*; **Mary Jo Gediman**, *This I Believe* Outreach Director; **Jay Allison**, host and curator of *This I Believe*; and **Denise Cronin** of Henry Holt.

The publisher also extends special thanks to the following individuals whose comments were instrumental in shaping this series:

Meghan Ackley, University of Texas, Austin, TX; **Frances Boyd**, Columbia University, New York, NY; **Norman Cain**, International House, Rome, Italy; **Jean Correll**, Wheaton High School, Wheaton, MD; **Robert Esser**, (ret.), Madison Area Technical College, Madison, Wisconsin; **Holly Fernalld**, Niwot High School, Niwot, CO; **Jennifer Gaudet**, Santa Ana School of Continuing Education, Santa Ana, CA; **Rebecca Haag**, International House, Rome, Italy; **Lisa Hockstein**, Westchester Community College, Valhalla, NY; **Kate Johnson**, Union County College, Elizabeth, NJ; **Tamara Jones**, Howard Community College, Columbia, MD; **Ronny Kempenich**, Wheaton high School, Wheaton, TX; **Sydney Lally**, Quincy High School, Quincy, MA; **Carol McBride**, Food and Agricultural Organization of the U.N., Language Training, Rome, Italy; **Kristin Ruopp Mena**, Montgomery Blair High School, Silver Springs, MD; **Anne Moore**, Food and Agricultural Organization of the U.N., Language Training, Rome, Italy; **Kim Newcomer**, University of Washington, Seattle, WA; **Delis Pitt**, Columbia University and New School University, New York, NY; **Theresa Sammarco**, Wootton High School, Rockville, MD; **Barbara Sarapata**, Columbia University and New School University, New York, NY; **Kelly Roberts Weibel**, Edmonds Community College, Lynnwood, WA; **David Wiese**, New York University and New School University, New York, NY; and students, **Moira Agrimi** and **Anna Riera**, Rome, Italy.

Also, many thanks to research assistant **John Kay Lee**.

SCOPE AND SEQUENCE

	UNIT	TOPIC	LANGUAGE
	UNIT 1 Finding Prosperity by Feeding Monkeys —Harold Taw	Practicing birthday rituals and other traditions	Time order words
	UNIT 2 In Praise of the "Wobblies" —Ted Gup	Being undecided	Expressions to show two sides of an issue
	UNIT 3 The Optimism of Jazz —Colleen Shaddox	Finding hope in music	Phrasal verbs
	UNIT 4 Always Go... —Deirdre Sullivan	Doing the right thing	Expressing satisfaction and regret in the past
	UNIT 5 The Making of Poems —Gregory Orr	Poetry; shaping experiences and overcoming isolation	Expressions for participating in a small group discussion
	UNIT 6 When Ordinary People Achieve Extraordinary Things —Jody Williams	Working with others to solve global problems	Expressions for keeping a conversation going

PRONUNCIATION	FUNCTION	SPEAKING TASK
Pauses with time order words	Describing a process	Describe a ritual, tradition, or routine
Showing contrast	Giving opinions	Present two sides of an issue and give your opinion
Word stress in phrasal verbs	Explaining preferences; describing and adding details	Present and describe a piece of music
Reductions with *have*	Expressing satisfaction and regret for past actions	Describe a time when you did or didn't do the right thing; explain the result and how you feel about it now.
Word stress: content words	Paraphrasing; facilitating small group discussions	Present a poem and explaining what it means to you; facilitate a group discussion of the poem
Intonation for surprise and doubt	Agreeing and offering additional ideas	Propose ways to solve a local or global problem

UNIT	TOPIC	LANGUAGE
UNIT 7 Disrupting my Comfort Zone —Brian Grazer	Challenging our daily routines to improve our creativity	*Recommend* and *suggest*
UNIT 8 A Goal of Service to Humankind —Anthony Fauci	Following one's guiding principles	Signposting language
UNIT 9 Creative Solutions to Life's Challenges —Frank X Walker	Celebrating creativity in everyday life	*Would* for repeated actions in the past
UNIT 10 Free Minds and Hearts at Work —Jackie Robinson	Overcoming obstacles	Future and future perfect
UNIT 11 In Giving I Connect with Others —Isabel Allende	The importance of giving to and connecting with others	Infinitives for describing hopes, desires, and actions
UNIT 12 A Balance between Nature and Nurture —Gloria Steinem	Looking at *nature* and *nurture*	Expressions for making strong arguments

PRONUNCIATION	FUNCTION	SPEAKING TASK
Unstressed schwa [ə]	Making recommendations and suggestions	Recommend specific ways of challenging our daily routines
Pauses with signposting expressions	Stating guiding principles and giving examples	Give a speech about one of your guiding principles
Contractions with *would*	Describing a person and giving examples to illustrate a point	Describe a creative person; give examples of past actions that demonstrate their creativity
Contractions with *will*	Making predictions and explaining opinions	Predict two problems society will overcome in the next 100 years
Reduction of *to*	Interviewing	Respond to questions about a volunteer experience; describe that experience
Word stress in transitions	Debating	Participate in a debate about *nature* vs. *nurture*

Glossary defines important lower-frequency words and expressions to support listening comprehension.

Connect to the Topic prepares students to listen by offering an early opportunity to engage in the topic and anticipate what they will hear in the essay.

UNIT 11

IN GIVING I CONNECT WITH OTHERS
–Isabel Allende

GETTING READY

CD 2 Track 30 Listen and read about the essayist.

Meet Isabel Allende

Isabel Allende was born in Peru and raised in Chile. She is best known for writing novels. Her personal philosophy of life has been shaped by her experiences with her family. One experience in particular made her write a book and this essay. Her daughter, Paula, died in 1992. After losing Paula, Allende realized an important belief. She applies this belief to her daily life.

Connect to the Topic

Discuss these questions with a partner.

- Isabel Allende's daughter, Paula, was a volunteer. She worked to help poor women and children.
- Do you (or does someone you know) volunteer to help others in the community? Where?
- If someone told you he or she wanted to volunteer, what kind of advice would you give that person?

GLOSSARY

You will hear these words and expressions in the essay. Read their definitions before you listen.

coma /ˈkoumə/ *n.* the condition of not being awake for a long time, usually after an accident or illness

agony /ˈægəni/ *n.* extreme pain or suffering

grieving /ˈgrivɪŋ/ *n.* feeling very sad for a period of time, usually after the death of a loved one

paralyzed /ˈpærəˌlaɪzd/ *adj.* not being able to move the body

let go (of) /lɛt gou əv/ *v.* stop holding someone or something

cling (to) /klɪŋ tu/ *v.* be dependent on someone or their beliefs

LISTENING
Listen for Main Ideas

CD 2 Track 31 Read this question and these sentences. Then listen to Isabel Allende's essay. Circle the letter of the answer to this question.

110

In Giving I Connect with Others **111**

Getting Ready introduces students to the essayist and provides necessary background as a starting point for the exploration of the speaker's core belief.

Listen for Main Ideas enables students to identify key points in the essay.

Listening strategically supports comprehension by providing purposeful opportunities to listen and explore the content.

Vocabulary for Comprehension

presents and practices useful, higher-frequency words and expressions to support listening comprehension and classroom interaction on the topic.

Listen for Details challenges
students to listen more closely, go deeper into the topic, and think critically.

Which statement best summarizes Allende's belief?

a. It's better to receive than to give.

b. Share your experiences, but within limits.

c. Giving is life's greatest joy and keeps our loved ones in our hearts.

d. People should volunteer to help their communities.

Vocabulary for Comprehension

CD 2 Track 33 Read and listen to the letter from the Women's and Children's Organization of Northern California. Discuss the meanings of the boldfaced words. Then match the words with their definitions on page 113.

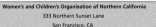

Women's and Children's Organization of Northern California
333 Northern Sunset Lane
San Francisco, CA

I am the assistant director of the Women's and Children's Organization of Northern California (WCONC). Last year, we received a $20,000 grant from the Isabel Allende Foundation. I would like to (a) **reflect on** how this grant has helped us.

First, our (b) **principles** have always included helping women and children when they most need it. Our director decided to reduce her salary to avoid shutting down a breakfast program for kids in school. With the grant money, we don't have to worry about eliminating our community programs any longer. The grant helps us keep (c) **consistency** in our programs: The WCONC can be there to help women and children when they need us most.

Second, the Isabel Allende Foundation has inspired our new (d) **mantra**: "There's no time like the present to give."

Finally, this grant allows us to reach out to women in difficult situations. These women often think they must remain (e) **independent**; often they don't trust others. We must reach out to them. We work with them to rebuild the lives they (f) **crave**: working and providing for their children while they participate in their communities in meaningful ways.

This has all been made possible by the hard work of our staff, and the Isabel Allende Foundation.

1. _____ relying only on themselves

2. _____ guiding ideas

3. _____ quality of always staying the same

4. _____ want very much

5. _____ repeated word or group of words

6. _____ think carefully and for a long time about something

Listen for Details

A **CD 2 Track 34** Read these sentences. Then listen to Allende's essay again. Check (✓) *True*, *False*, or *Don't Know*.

Sentence	True	False	Don't Know
1. Allende thought about her beliefs during her daughter's illness.	☑	☐	☐
2. Before Paula's illness, Allende didn't think about her beliefs much.	☐	☐	☐
3. According to Allende, you have to give so you can feel a variety of feelings.	☐	☐	☐
4. As a volunteer, Allende's daughter, Paula, needed lots of things.	☐	☐	☐
5. Since her daughter's death, Allende no longer clings to anything.	☐	☐	☐
6. Allende prefers to give rather than to receive.	☐	☐	☐
7. Allende's family and dog don't like her.	☐	☐	☐
8. According to Allende, spending money is a way of showing love.	☐	☐	☐

Reacting to the Essay

invites students to think critically and apply the ideas in the essay to their own experience and beliefs.

BUILD FLUENCY

Language teaches and practices important language functions or structures needed for success in the final speaking task.

Speaking presents a variety of engaging speaking tasks designed to develop fluency and confidence in speaking English.

B `CD 2 Track 35` Read these sentences. Listen to the essay again. Does Allende mention these examples of giving? Circle *Yes* or *No*.

1. taking care of her daughter at home	Yes	No
2. advising women with children on legal issues	Yes	No
3. spending time teaching computer skills to the elderly	Yes	No
4. sharing experience, knowledge, talent, and wealth	Yes	No

REACTING TO THE ESSAY

Discuss your answers to these questions.

1. When talking about her family, Allende says, "I adore my husband, my son, my grandchildren, my mother, my dog, and frankly I don't know if they even like me. But who cares? Loving them is my joy." What do you think about Allende's attitude? Is this a good attitude to have toward those you love? Explain.

2. Allende gives by telling stories. What other ways can people give in the way that Allende talks about?

3. In which professions is it important to be a giver? For example, can a person be a good nurse if she or he is not giving? Explain.

BACKGROUND NOTES

Read the timeline highlighting some events in Isabel Allende's life.

1942	She is born in Lima, Peru, where her father, Tomás, was Chilean ambassador
1963	Her daughter Paula is born.
1967	She begins her writing career.
1982	Her first novel *House of the Spirits* is published in Spain.
1992	Paula passes away.
1994	*Paula*, a memoir of Isabel's early life, is published in Spain.
1996	The Isabel Allende Foundation is formed in memory of her daughter.

Isabel Allende **and her husband Willie Gordon**

Today, Isabel Allende and her husband live in San Francisco, CA, near her son, Nicolás, and his family.

114 UNIT 11

SPEAKING

Isabel Allende's mantra is "You only have what you give." The life her daughter chose as a volunteer inspired Allende to give more of herself. In this section, you will interview each other about your own or others' volunteer experience.

Build Fluency

Language: Infinitives

Some verbs and verb phrases are followed by the infinitive (*to* + base form of verb).

EXPLAINING ACTIONS: INFINITIVES	
Verb + infinitive:	EXAMPLES:
hope	As a volunteer, Laura *hopes* to help many poor families.
want	She *wants* to volunteer six days a week.
decide	Laura *decided* to help them because she knew no one else would.
find time	She always *finds time* to spend with poor families.
have an opportunity	People are happy they *have an opportunity* to work with Laura.
Verb + object + infinitive:	EXAMPLES:
inspire	Laura's parents *inspired* her to volunteer.
encourage	They *encouraged* her to donate her time and talent.
expect	She *expected* them to help when possible.

In Giving I Connect with Others 115

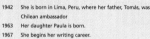

Culture Notes and **Background Notes** give insight into historical and cultural references in the essay.

BUILD FLUENCY

Pronunciation provides instruction and practice in pronunciation, stress, and intonation in preparation for the final speaking task.

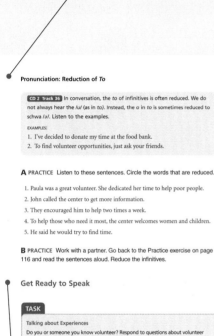

Pronunciation: Reduction of *To*

CD 2 Track 36 In conversation, the *to* of infinitives is often reduced. We do not always hear the /u/ (as in *to*). Instead, the o in *to* is sometimes reduced to schwa /ə/. Listen to the examples.

EXAMPLES:
1. I've decided to donate my time at the food bank.
2. To find volunteer opportunities, just ask your friends.

A PRACTICE Listen to these sentences. Circle the words that are reduced.

1. Paula was a great volunteer. She dedicated her time to help poor people.
2. John called the center to get more information.
3. They encouraged him to help two times a week.
4. To help those who need it most, the center welcomes women and children.
5. He said he would try to find time.

B PRACTICE Work with a partner. Go back to the Practice exercise on page 116 and read the sentences aloud. Reduce the infinitives.

Get Ready to Speak

> **TASK**
>
> Talking about Experiences
> Do you or someone you know volunteer? Respond to questions about volunteer experiences. Tell others about those experiences.

1. Take three minutes. Make notes about your or another person's volunteer experience. What kind of work is it? Why did you or someone you know decide to volunteer?
2. Interview a partner about volunteering.

> 1. What kind of volunteer work is it?
> 2. Why did you or someone you know decide to volunteer?
> 3. How do you or someone you know find the time to volunteer?
> 4. Did anyone inspire you or someone you know to volunteer?
> 5. What would you say to encourage others to volunteer?

Use these expressions, or interjections to respond to comments. Then move on to the next topic.

> **USEFUL EXPRESSIONS**
> **Responding to Comments**
>
> Really? How interesting. Now . . .
> That's amazing. So . . .
> Wow! What a story. My next question . . .

3. Organize your ideas. Insert verbs and infinitives where necessary. Practice giving your talk to another pair of students. Each partner should speak for about the same amount of time. Make changes as needed.

Remember to:
- use verbs and infinitives.
- reduce the pronunciation of the *to* of infinitives.
- use the useful expressions when responding to people's comments.

Get Ready to Speak guides students through steps to complete the final speaking task.

Writing gives students an opportunity to recast their ideas in written form, allowing them to go deeper, give personal insights, and receive valuable feedback from their teacher.

Speak prompts students when and how to deliver their response to the speaking task.

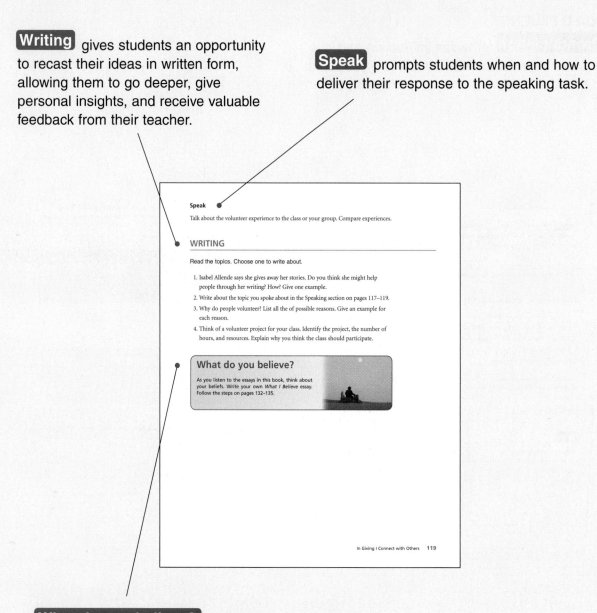

Speak

Talk about the volunteer experience to the class or your group. Compare experiences.

WRITING

Read the topics. Choose one to write about.

1. Isabel Allende says she gives away her stories. Do you think she might help people through her writing? How? Give one example.
2. Write about the topic you spoke about in the Speaking section on pages 117–119.
3. Why do people volunteer? List all of possible reasons. Give an example for each reason.
4. Think of a volunteer project for your class. Identify the project, the number of hours, and resources. Explain why you think the class should participate.

What do you believe?

As you listen to the essays in this book, think about your beliefs. Write your own *What I Believe* essay. Follow the steps on pages 132–135.

In Giving I Connect with Others   119

What do you believe? guides students through the planning, writing, and delivery of their own *What I Believe* essay.

FINDING PROSPERITY BY FEEDING MONKEYS
–Harold Taw

GETTING READY

CD 1 Track 2 Listen and read about the essayist.

> ### Meet Harold Taw
>
> Harold Taw was born into a very poor family in Burma.[1] When he was born, a Buddhist monk predicted that Taw's birth would bring the family great prosperity, or success. However, to ensure this prosperity, the Buddhist monk said that Taw must follow a ritual, or tradition, every year on his birthday.

[1]also called Myanmar

1

Connect to the Topic

Discuss this question with a partner.

What are some birthday rituals or traditions you or people you know follow?

> ### GLOSSARY
>
> You will hear these words and expressions in the essay. Read their definitions before you listen.
>
> **do** (something) **without fail** /du wɪ ðaʊt feɪl/ *idiom* make sure to always do something
>
> **superstitious** /supɚ'stɪʃəs/ *adj.* believing that some objects or actions bring good or bad luck
>
> **karmic** /kɑrmɪk/ *adj.* related to the idea that your actions will bring similar results in the future; **karma** *n.*
>
> **narcissism** /'nɑrsə, sɪzəm/ *n.* thinking about or liking oneself too much
>
> **the coast is clear** /ðə koʊst əz klɪr/ *idiom* when you are free to do something because no one will see you do it
>
> **make an exception** /meɪk ən ɪk'sɛpʃən/ *exp.* change the rules for someone in a special situation
>
> **collective bargaining agreement** /kə'lɛktɪv 'bɑrgənɪŋ ə'grimənt/ *n.* an agreement between employers and workers about job conditions

LISTENING

Listen for Main Ideas

CD 1 Track 3 Read these sentences. Then listen to Harold Taw's essay. Circle the letter of the answer that best completes each sentence.

1. Taw's family now lives in _____.

   a. Burma   b. the United States

2. The Buddhist monk told him to _____ monkeys every year on his birthday.

   a. feed   b. visit

3. The monk said that performing this ritual would ensure his family's

   _____.

   a. prosperity   b. poverty

4. Following this ritual has been _____ for Taw.

   a. easy   b. challenging

5. Today Taw _____ the ritual.

   a. still performs   b. has stopped performing

Woman feeding a monkey at a zoo

Vocabulary for Comprehension

CD 1 Track 5 Read and listen to these passages. Then match the boldfaced words and expressions with their definitions below.

1. Do you have money troubles? Don't worry! You *can* (a) **overcome** your financial problems, and we can help. Call Money Solutions today. It is possible to find (b) **prosperity** if you are careful with your money. Let us help you. If you are smart today, money will not be a (c) **burden** in the future. Call us.

_b_ financial success

_____ fight and win against

_____ something heavy that makes you worry

2. Children who live in (d) **poverty** do not have the same chances as other children. For example, poor children often do not eat well. Therefore, they do not get the (e) **nourishment** they need to grow and live well. Without good nutrition, they will not grow up strong and (f) **flourish**.

_____ grow and develop well

_____ food

_____ having no money or possessions

3. Performing his birthday ritual has been a challenge. Once Taw secretly brought (g) **contraband** peanuts to a zoo and threw them to the monkeys. Because zoos and zookeepers do not let people feed the animals, (h) **violating** zoo rules was sometimes necessary. Another time, he asked to feed a man's pet monkey, but this man didn't believe him. The man (i) **suspected** Taw of wanting to free his monkey. The man thought Taw's story about his birthday ritual was just a (j) **ploy** to let his monkey go free.

_____ trick to gain an advantage in a situation

_____ disobeying or breaking

_____ something illegally taken in or out of a place

_____ thought he was guilty of doing something bad

Listen for Details

A `CD 1 Track 6` Read the chart. Then listen to Taw's essay again. Circle the word or phrase in parentheses that correctly completes each statement in the chart.

Event	Details
Living in Burma	1. The monk did not want the ritual to be a (tradition / burden).
Living in America	2. Sometimes he had to (violate / follow) rules to feed monkeys.
	3. He learned (English / Burmese) from bad TV.
Going to the zoo as a boy	4. They went (early in the morning / late at night).
	5. Harold would throw the contraband peanuts when (the coast was clear / the zoo was closed).
Going to the zoo on his 18th birthday	6. He went with his (father / friends).
	7. They arrived ten minutes (early / late).
	8. Taw asked a zookeeper to (make an exception / find a pet store).
	9. She (agreed / did not agree).
Feeding monkeys on other birthdays	10. A friend who trains monkeys for the movies let Taw (feed / visit) his monkeys.
	11. A man with a pet monkey thought Taw wanted to (free / feed) it.

	12. One time, he managed to feed a marmoset[1] being kept in a (box / birdcage) at a pet store.
	13. He had to wear a (bathing suit / biohazard suit) at a laboratory.
Feeding monkeys every year since he was born	14. It's not (easy / enjoyable), but somehow he finds a way to feed a monkey every year on his birthday.

B **CD 1 Track 7** Read these sentences. Then listen to the essay again. Write *T* (true) or *F* (false).

——— 1. He thinks that the ritual might sound superstitious to some people.

——— 2. According to the tradition, Taw's family must think about him on his birthday.

——— 3. When Taw feeds monkeys, someone from his family must go with him.

——— 4. Taw continues to feed monkeys on his birthday only at zoos.

——— 5. For Taw, feeding monkeys is a way for him to show he honors his family.

REACTING TO THE ESSAY

Discuss your answers to these questions.

1. Do you think that Harold is ensuring his family's prosperity when he feeds monkeys on his birthday?

2. Taw says the monk didn't mean for the ritual to be a burden. How would you feel about performing this ritual? Do you think it's a burden or not? Explain.

3. Taw says that he believes in honoring his family any way he can. In what ways do other people honor their families?

[1]a type of monkey found in Latin and South America

CULTURE NOTES

In his essay, Harold Taw mentions the following movie and activists. Read about them to help you understand the essay better.

Out of Africa: a 1985 Hollywood movie about Westerners living in Africa

animal rights activists: people who publicly protest for fair treatment of animals

Animal rights activists

SPEAKING

Harold Taw has performed his birthday ritual every year since his birth. He says he has faith in his family and believes in honoring that faith any way he can. In this section, you will plan and give a presentation about a ritual, tradition, or routine that you follow, or one that someone you know follows.

Build Fluency

Language: Time Order Words

To describe rituals, traditions, or routines, use time order words with the simple present. This helps make the order of events clear. Read these sentences with time order words. Notice where the comma (,) is in each sentence.

Describing a Ritual, Tradition, or Routine	
TIME ORDER WORDS	**Examples:**
first, second (etc.)	**First,** Taw ensures he has some peanuts.
	Second, he goes to the zoo.
next, then, after that	**Next,** Harold makes sure the coast is clear.
	Then, he throws his contraband peanuts to the monkeys.
	After that, he takes a walk.

before	**Before** he celebrates his birthday, he looks for a monkey to feed.
as soon as	**As soon as** he feeds a monkey, he leaves.
when	**When** he has problems feeding monkeys in one place, he looks for another.
while	**While** he is getting ready to feed monkeys at zoos, he looks around to see if the coast is clear.
finally	**Finally**, he goes home to celebrate with his family.

PRACTICE In each sentence, one time order word is not correct. Cross out the incorrect time order word in parentheses.

1. (First, / As soon as / When) my grandfather wakes up, he makes some coffee.

2. (When / Then, / Next,) he reads the newspaper and does some exercises.

3. (After that, / As soon as / Next,) he prepares his breakfast.

4. He gets dressed (when / third / as soon as) he finishes eating.

5. (While / Finally,) he is washing the dishes, he sings a song.

6. (Next, / Then, / As soon as) he gets his briefcase ready.

7. He turns on his cell phone (before / while) he is putting on his coat.

8. (While / After that, / Finally,) he locks the door and takes the bus to work.

1. Read the questions on the Worksheet that follows. Then answer the questions about the ritual, tradition, or routine you are going to speak about. Include as many details as you can.

Worksheet: My Ritual, Tradition, or Routine

1. What is the ritual, tradition, or routine?

2. Who observes it?

3. When and where is it observed?

4. What are the steps in the ritual, tradition, or routine?

   • First, . . .

   • Then, . . .

5. Why do you / does the person follow it? What is its meaning?

6. What do you / does the person hope the result will be?

2. Review the information on your worksheet and put the ideas in the best order. Then, describe your ritual, tradition, or routine to a partner.

Remember to:
• use time order words.
• pause as needed.

Speak

Present your ritual, tradition, or routine. When you have finished speaking, take questions from your audience.

Pronunciation: Pauses with Time Order Words

CD 1 Track 8 A pause is a short time when you stop doing something. When speaking, a pause can help to make ideas clear. Pause at the end of a phrase or clause that begins with a time order word. In writing, this pause is marked with a comma. Time order words near the end of sentences do not have a comma, and there is no pause in speaking. Listen to the examples.

EXAMPLES: **Before playing in a football game**, (pause) my brother always follows a good-luck ritual.

My brother always follows a good-luck ritual **before playing in a football game**. (no pause)

A PRACTICE Listen and repeat these sentences with time order words.

1. After he wakes up, Jay always follows the same routine.
2. He drinks a glass of water first.
3. Second, he stretches for ten minutes.
4. He makes tea next. While the water is boiling, he reads the paper.
5. Finally, he takes a shower and gets dressed.

B PRACTICE Write out five sentences from the Practice exercise on page 8. Work with a partner. Take turns saying the sentences. Use pauses where necessary.

Get Ready to Speak

TASK

Describing the Steps in a Ritual, Tradition, or Routine

Give a presentation about a ritual, tradition, or routine that you or someone you know follows. Describe the process, and explain why you or this person follow it.

WRITING

Read these topics. Choose one to write about.

1. For Taw, following his birthday ritual shows his family that he honors them. Describe one specific way you can honor your family. Use time order words if necessary.

2. Do you think Taw will want his children to follow a birthday ritual? Give reasons to explain your answer.

3. Write a letter to Harold Taw. Tell him your reaction to his birthday ritual.

What do you believe?

As you listen to the essays in this book, think about your beliefs. Write your own *What I Believe* essay. Follow the steps on pages 132–135.

WRITING

Read these topics. Choose one to write about.

1. For Taw, following his birthday ritual shows his family that he honors them. Describe one specific way you can honor your family. Use time order words if necessary.

2. Do you think Taw will want his children to follow a birthday ritual? Give reasons to explain your answer.

3. Write a letter to Harold Taw. Tell him your reaction to his birthday ritual.

What do you believe?

As you listen to the essays in this book, think about your beliefs. Write your own *What I Believe* essay. Follow the steps on pages 132–135.

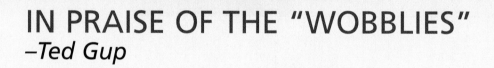

UNIT 2

IN PRAISE OF THE "WOBBLIES"
–Ted Gup

GETTING READY

CD 1 Track 9 Listen and read about the essayist.

Meet Ted Gup

Ted Gup is a journalist. At the beginning of his career, he tried to get an internship[1] at the *Washington Post* newspaper. To choose the right person for the internship, the editor of the *Post* had a lunch meeting with ten finalists, including Gup and some students from Harvard University. At lunch, they discussed the "hot" issues of the day. The Harvard students expressed clear arguments, or reasons, for their opinions. Gup's opinions were not clear at all. He was "on the fence" about many issues. He was "wobbly." One month later, Gup received a rejection letter. The letter said that he did not get the internship, but the editor liked his attitude very much.

[1] a job a person does for professional experience but for little pay

Connect to the Topic

Discuss these questions with a partner.

Gup was "wobbly" on certain issues. Think about this example: Imagine that you recently saw a classmate cheat on an important test.

- What are the issues for and against telling the teacher about the cheating?
- Why might some people be wobbly on this issue?

GLOSSARY

You will hear these words and expressions in the essay. Read their definitions before you listen.

A reporter asking about an issue

opposing arguments /əˈpoʊzɪŋ ˈɑrgyəments/ *n.* two very different sides or opinions on an issue

no man's land /ˈnoʊ mænz lænd/ *exp.* the place between two opposing sides

have a hunch /ˈhəv ə ˈhʌntʃ/ *exp.* have a guess or feeling about something, but you do not know for sure

know where (one) stands /noʊ wɛr wʌn stændz/ *idiom* have a clear opinion about something

muddled /ˈmʌdld/ *adj.* confused; also **perplexed** /pɚˈplɛkst/ *adj.*

torn /tɔrn/ *adj.* undecided, unable to make a decision

common ground /ˈkɑmən graʊnd/ *exp.* a point on which everyone agrees

inquire /ɪnˈkwaɪɚ/ *v.* ask someone for information

inquisitive /ɪnˈkwɪzəṭɪv/ *adj.* wanting to find out more information

LISTENING

Listen for Main Ideas

CD 1 Track 10 Read these sentences. Then listen to Ted Gup's essay. Circle the letter of the answer that best completes each sentence.

1. This essay is about _____.

   a. getting a job at a newspaper   b. feeling comfortable with confusion

2. Over the years, Gup _____.

   a. became clear about hot issues   b. accepted his confusion

3. A wobbly is a person who _____.

   a. is not certain about issues   b. has clear opinions about issues

Vocabulary for Comprehension

CD 1 Track 12 Read and listen to these sentences. Then circle the letter of the word or phrase closest in meaning to the boldfaced word or expression.

1. I was **yearning for** some experience at a newspaper. I was almost finished with school and ready to work.

   a. afraid of

   b. wanting something very much

2. I went for a job interview last week. The interviewers asked some really difficult questions. My answers weren't very good, so I think I lost my **shot** at the position.

   a. opportunity

   b. nervousness

3. At my job interview, the interviewer thought my ideas had a lot of **merit**. She was so impressed that she offered me the job.

   a. value

   b. errors

4. My daughter got an internship because she kept on **bugging** the people in the human resources department. She called them at least once a week to show her interest.

   a. paying

   b. asking

5. My friend worked part-time for *The Los Angeles Times*, but this year the paper **hired** him as a full-time employee.

   a. gave a job to

   b. refused to give a job to

6. My boss gave me a project to do last year. She was so happy with my work that she has given me **license** to decide what my next project will be.

   a. money

   b. freedom

7. In comparison to my older brother, I feel **inadequate**. He has achieved so much more than I have.

   a. not good enough

   b. very confident

8. I **envy** Mary. She seems so happy with her new job. I wish I enjoyed my job as much!

   a. am similar to

   b. am jealous of

9. It has taken many years, but I have decided to **embrace** my shyness. I can't speak in front of a lot of people. However, I can talk to lots of different people individually, and that's good enough.

   a. accept

   b. fight against

10. I don't like to **crusade** to make everyone believe what I believe. People should have their own opinions.

    a. cry

    b. fight

11. Some people think I'm **quirky** because I wear crazy fashions, but after they talk to me, they see that we're not very different.

    a. unusual

    b. not very intelligent

Listen for Details

A `CD 1 Track 13` Read these questions. Then listen to Gup's essay again. Circle the letter of the best answer to each question.

1. Why did the *Washington Post* editor reject Gup for the internship?

    a. He was confused.   c. He was too young.

    b. He was open-minded.   d. He was too clear.

2. What did the editor at the *Washington Post* do?

    a. He hired Gup eventually.   c. He gave Gup some bad advice.

    b. He told Gup to choose a new career.   d. He told Gup to be more confident.

3. Another editor at the *Washington Post* once told Gup that he was "wobbly." According to the editor's description, which of the following is <u>not</u> a quality of a wobbly:

    a. open-minded   c. confused

    b. inquisitive   d. passionate

B CD 1 Track 14 Read these questions. Then listen to the essay again. Write your answers to the questions.

1. Summarize how Gup felt about his confusion thirty-five years ago and how he feels about it today. How did his attitude toward his confusion change?

2. What did the editor's rejection letter to Gup say? How did Gup react to the letter?

3. Why do you think the editor at the *Post* eventually hired Gup?

4. In his essay, Gup says, "But in periods of crisis, when passions are high and certainty runs rabid,[1] it's good to have a few of us on hand. In such times, I believe it falls to us wobblies to try and hold the shrinking common ground." According to Gup, why are wobblies important?

REACTING TO THE ESSAY

Discuss your answers to these questions.

1. Look back at your answers to the questions in the Connect to the Topic section on page 13. Were you wobbly on the cheating issue? Explain.

2. In his essay, Gup says he believes that there are times when it's good to have a few wobblies around. Do you agree? Explain.

3. Gup says that as a wobbly, he usually finds degrees of merit in both sides of an issue. Do you usually see both sides of an issue, or are you more likely to take one side or the other?

[1]moves fast and uncontrolled

The 1960s and early 1970s were a time of disagreement and change in the United States. Read the notes related to this time, which Gup mentions in his essay.

Vietnam War: a war that lasted from 1954 to 1975. The United States joined South Vietnam from 1961 to 1972 to fight against North Vietnam. More than a million Vietnamese, including many civilians, and over 50,000 Americans died. This was the longest and most unpopular military conflict in American history.

President Nixon: controversial U.S. president from 1969 to 1974.

demonstrations: public gatherings of groups of people to show disagreement with a government or business; protests. In the late 1960s and early 1970s, demonstrations against the Vietnam War were common.

Vietnam War protesters in front of the White House on November 30, 1965

SPEAKING

In his essay, Ted Gup states his belief that having a clear opinion on every issue is not always necessary. What is important is to understand the different sides of an argument and to know when you are unsure. In this section, you will present a hot issue at your school or in the news.

Build Fluency

Language: Showing Two Sides of an Issue

To show two sides of an issue or to show contrast between two things, use the following expressions.

SHOWING TWO SIDES OF AN ISSUE	
Expressions	**Examples:**
Use *On the one hand . . .* and *On the other hand . . .* to show two sides of a single issue or topic.	Topic: the prime minister's job performance

Use these expressions together. Each expression begins a sentence.	**On the one hand,** *the prime minister* has made some good changes. **On the other hand,** *she* has made some bad mistakes.
Use *whereas* to show contrast between two topics. Use *whereas* at the beginning of a sentence, or in the middle.	Two topics: Elena and her sister **Whereas** *Elena* is very hopeful about the future, *her sister* is not optimistic.
Whereas is formal in speaking. It is often used in writing.	*Elena* is hopeful about the future, **whereas** *her sister* is not.

Other examples to consider:

- **On the one hand**, learning a foreign language is useful. **On the other hand**, it is time consuming.
- **On the one hand**, I think Paris has too many people. **On the other hand**, the diversity of people makes Paris very interesting.
- **Whereas** the city of Paris is busy and large, Tours, France, is small and quiet.
- The city of Tours, France, is small and quiet, **whereas** Paris is busy and large.

A PRACTICE Match the sentence beginnings on the left with their endings on the right.

_c_ 1. In the United States you must have insurance to get health care,

a. small towns have clean air.

_____ 2. On the one hand, hybrid cars are better for the environment than regular cars.

b. On the other hand, they leave out many details.

_____ 3. Whereas large cities are polluted,

c. whereas in Spain it is paid for by the government.

_____ 4. On the one hand, historical movies help people understand the past.

d. On the other hand, they cost more money.

B PRACTICE Answer these questions using the information in parentheses and the correct expressions for showing two sides of an issue.

1. A: What do you think of hybrid cars?

    B: (*better for the environment / cost more*)

    On the one hand, hybrid cars are better for the environment. On the
    other hand, they cost more.

2. A: What's your opinion: Should kids have cell phones in high school?

    B: (*useful in emergencies / distracting*)

    _____

3. A: Does it take you a long time to commute to work?

    B: It depends. (*the train takes thirty-five minutes / going by car takes twenty minutes*)

    _____

4. A: Some people think young children should learn to use computers in school.

    B: (*computers are helpful / learning how to read and write must come first*)

    _____

Pronunciation: Showing Contrast

CD 1 Track 15 Use correct word stress to show contrast when discussing two sides of an issue or comparing two things. Stress the words that show contrast or emphasize a difference. Listen to the example.

EXAMPLE: On the **one** hand, big cities offer **many** things to do. On the **other** hand, they are **too crowded**.

A [CD 1 Track 15] PRACTICE Listen to these sentences and repeat them. Stress the words that show contrast or emphasize a difference.

- Whereas **big cities** have **many** museums, **small towns** might have only **one** or **none**.
- **Big cities** have **many** museums, whereas **small towns** might have only **one** or **none**.
- On the **one** hand, learning English is **difficult**. On the **other** hand, it's very **important** to me.

B PRACTICE Work with a partner. Go back to the Practice exercises on pages 19–20. Mark the words that show contrast or emphasize a difference. Then take turns reading the sentences with correct stress.

Get Ready to Speak

TASK

Showing Two Sides of an Issue

Choose a hot topic in your school or in the news. With a partner, present the different sides of the issue. Include details you are still unsure about. Give your opinion on the issue or explain why you are "on the fence."

1. Work with a partner. Brainstorm a list of five hot issues in your school or in the news. Choose one that you both want to speak about.
2. Identify the different sides of the issue. Organize your ideas in the chart. Discuss and note anything that is still unclear to you.

Issue: _____	
Side 1: _____	Side 2: _____
_____	_____
_____	_____

<u>Note</u>: If there are more than two possible sides, draw this chart in your notebook and add more boxes.

3. Plan which partner will say what. Make sure you both speak for the same amount of time.

4. Work with another pair of students. Practice presenting your issue to the other pair (your audience). Make changes as needed.

Remember to:

- use the expressions for showing two sides of an issue or for showing contrast.

- use correct word stress for comparing and contrasting.

Speak

Work with a different pair of students. Give your presentation. When you have finished speaking, take questions from your audience.

WRITING

Read these topics. Choose one to write about.

1. Write about the hot issue you spoke about in the Speaking section on pages 21–22. List the different sides of the issue. Then explain why you are or are not wobbly about this issue.

2. Do you think it is better for a journalist to be a wobbly or to have very clear opinions about issues? Explain.

3. In journalism, it can be argued that it is important to consider both sides of an argument. In what other professions besides journalism is it important to see both sides of an issue? Identify at least two professions. Explain your choices.

What do you believe?

As you listen to the essays in this book, think about your beliefs. Write your own *What I Believe* essay. Follow the steps on pages 132–135.

THE OPTIMISM OF JAZZ
–Colleen Shaddox

GETTING READY

CD 1 Track 16 Listen and read about the essayist.

Meet Colleen Shaddox

Colleen Shaddox believes that jazz music can teach us important things about life. Jazz gave her happiness as a child, and comfort as an adult with cancer. Jazz has been present in her family for generations. She believes that it encourages people to be optimistic, or positive, when life gets difficult.

Connect to the Topic

Discuss these questions with a partner.

1. What is your favorite type of music?

   classical   disco   techno   rhythm and blues

   jazz   reggae   hip-hop   other

2. Why do you enjoy this music?

GLOSSARY

You will hear these words and expressions in the essay. Read their definitions before you listen.

Musical Terms

baby grand /ˈbeɪ bi grænd/ *n.* small version of a concert piano

vibrations /vaɪ ˈbreɪʃənz/ *n.* small movements resulting from loud noises or sounds

notes /noʊts/ *n.* individual musical sounds

sax /sæks/ *n.* saxophone, a brass wind instrument

sit in /ˈsɪt ɪn/ *v.* participate

jazz standard /ˈdʒæz ˈstændəd/ *exp.* a well-known piece of jazz music

A man with a saxophone

LISTENING

Listen for Main Ideas

CD 1 Track 17 Read these questions. Then listen to Colleen Shaddox's essay. Write your answers to the questions.

1. Who introduced Shaddox to jazz?

2. What did her son know?

3. What is one reason why Shaddox believes in jazz?

Vocabulary for Comprehension

CD 1 Track 19 Read and listen to these sentences. Then match the boldfaced words and expressions with their definitions below.

_c_ 1. My friend felt **despair** when she learned she had cancer. She couldn't think about the future and became depressed.

____ 2. Music can **lift** us **up** and help us think more positively.

____ 3. In America, African-Americans were **enslaved** from 1619 to 1865. They were owned by their masters and made to work for no money.

____ 4. To make a bicycle, a **welder** uses heat to put metal pieces together. Welders wear masks to protect their faces from the heat.

____ 5. My friend took a **detour** on the way home. She didn't go the usual way because of the heavy traffic.

____ 6. The challenges of medical school **tested** Jana's **faith** in her abilities. She almost gave up and quit school, but eventually she got her medical degree.

____ 7. When my friend lost her three-year-old son in a busy department store, she felt **terrified**.

____ 8. **I'll wager** that she felt really happy and thankful when she found her son.

____ 9. Parents who get angry at kids without asking the right questions think they have the **moral high ground**. They think the kids are always wrong.

____ 10. It seems like the **universe** has a way of bringing people together sometimes.

a. extremely afraid

b. a way of going that is different from the usual way

c. a feeling of having no hope

d. believing one is always right

e. said when you think something is true or likely

f. made someone doubt

g. someone who joins metal pieces together with fire

h. all of space, including all of the stars and planets, and everything that happens there

i. forced to work for someone else and not get paid

j. improve a mood

Listen for Details

A `CD 1 Track 20` Read these sentences. Then listen to Shaddox's essay again. Circle the letter of the answer that best completes each sentence.

1. Jazz was important to Shaddox as a child because her Uncle Charlie
   _____.

   a. taught her how to play the piano

   b. took her travelling around the world to jazz shows

   c. let her lie under the piano as he practiced

   d. gave her advice about life

2. Uncle Charlie played the piano at his night job even if he had
   _____.

   a. no time to practice

   b. tiny burns on his fingers from his welding job

   c. to clean the bathrooms at the club

   d. to perform at the Brooklyn Navy Yard

3. Shaddox says that jazz is "dogma-free" and that we can't predict where it will take us. According to Shaddox, this fact _____.

   a. forces us to have faith

   b. makes the music hard to follow

   c. makes us happy

   d. takes too many detours

4. When Shaddox's son sang the first few notes of a song called *Blue Dolphin Street*, she realized that _____.

   a. her son might have a difficult life without her

   b. she couldn't ever really leave her son

   c. her uncle Charlie would take care of her son

   d. not many three-year-olds know that song

5. As an adult with cancer, Shaddox felt _____ .

   a. like crying all the time

   b. better knowing that jazz connected her to her family

   c. extremely angry at her doctors

   d. terrified that her son would never know jazz music

6. On bad days, Shaddox puts on some jazz music and _____ .

   a. sings along with the songs

   b. calls her uncle Charlie

   c. feels sad all day long

   d. stays hopeful

B **CD 1 Track 21** Read these questions. Then listen to the essay again. Write your answers to the questions.

1. How does Shaddox feel about her Uncle Charlie?

   _____

2. Shaddox says "even songs that take you to despair lift you." What does she mean by this?

   _____

3. Shaddox went on a walk in the woods with her son. What happened on that walk?

   _____

4. How does jazz help Shaddox deal with negative news and bad events?

   _____

5. Which statement would Shaddox most likely say? Circle the letter of your choice. Explain.

   a. "Jazz is understood best by people who have studied music for years."

   b. "Jazz is a kind of music that anyone and everyone can listen to."

   _____

REACTING TO THE ESSAY

Discuss your answers to these questions.

1. Shaddox believes that jazz can give us hope when we are faced with difficulties in life. What other things in life besides music can help us go on?

2. Shaddox says that as a child she listened to her uncle practice piano, and that she felt very happy. Do you remember something that made you very happy as a child? Explain.

3. Shaddox realizes that jazz connects her with her son and with her uncle Charlie. What is something specific that bonds you and your family (or your groups of friends) together? Explain.

CULTURE NOTES

Jazz is difficult to describe. It is a style of music created by African-Americans in the United States. Jazz has strong rhythms and expresses deep emotion. There are parts for groups to play together and parts for musicians to play solo. Some jazz is carefully planned, but sometimes jazz musicians just start playing and let the music fly with their feelings.

In her essay, Colleen Shaddox mentions these famous jazz musicians:

A jazz band

Oscar Peterson, (1925–2007) composer and performer

Louis Armstrong, (1901–1971) composer of "Green Onions"

George Gershwin, (1898–1937) composer of *Rhapsody in Blue*

Miles Davis, (1926–1991) composer of "A Sunday Kind of Love"

Wynton Marsalis, (1961–) composer of "The Dirty Boogie"

SPEAKING

In her essay, Colleen Shaddox states that jazz music helps her understand and face life's challenges. In this section, you will present a piece of music and explain why you like it.

Build Fluency

Language: Phrasal Verbs

Shaddox uses phrasal verbs to describe what jazz means to her. You can use phrasal verbs to talk about your piece of music as well. Read these charts.

PHRASAL VERBS	
A phrasal verb is made up of a verb + particle. Particles look like prepositions, but they are part of the verb. Particles change the meaning of the verb.	EXAMPLE: She was **fighting back** tears.
Phrasal verbs can be transitive or intransitive. Transitive phrasal verbs have direct objects. Intransitive phrasal verbs do not have an object.	EXAMPLES: direct object She **fought back** *tears*. The song **caught on**. Everyone was singing it!

Most transitive phrasal verbs are separable. Direct objects that are nouns can come after the verb + particle, or between the verb and particle.
 	
Note: If the direct object is a pronoun, the pronoun must come between the verb and particle.
	EXAMPLES:
	
	                direct object
	She **turned up** *the volume*.
	
	             direct object
	She **turned** *the volume* **up**.
	
	I like this song. Please **turn** *it* **up**.

Some phrasal verbs are inseparable. Noun and pronoun objects always go after the verb + particle.	EXAMPLE: I had a hard time, but the music helped me **get through** *it*.

COMMON SEPARABLE PHRASAL VERBS	COMMON INSEPARABLE PHRASAL VERBS
cheer up *tr.* cause to feel happier	**catch on** *intr.* become popular
pick out *tr.* choose	**come from** *tr.* be from a place
put on *tr.* (music) begin to play a CD or tape	**get by** *intr.* survive
	get through *tr.* reach the end of a difficult situation
shut out *tr.* block; not hear or see	
turn on *tr.* start (something electric)	**stay up** *intr.* stay awake
turn up *tr.* increase the volume	**work out** *intr.* exercise (at the gym)
work out *tr.* solve (a problem or puzzle)	**turn out** *intr.* have a particular result

PRACTICE Read these sentences. Write *C* for correct or *I* for incorrect. Correct the incorrect sentences. Rewrite them on a separate piece of paper.

_C_ 1. Whenever I am sad or stressed, I pick out some music I like.

_____ 2. I love the group ABBA. The group comes from Sweden.

_____ 3. I come home, find an ABBA CD, press "Play," and turn it up loud!

_____ 4. Walking around the city, I listen to music. It helps me shut out all the noise.

_____ 5. When I need to think clearly, I listen to music. It helps me work my problems out.

_____ 6. At work, music helps me relax and clear my mind. I come up some good ideas with.

_____ 7. Music from the 1980s cheers up me.

_____ 8. I listen to music while I work out at the gym.

_____ 9. Above all, music helps me put the demands of life up with.

Pronunciation: Stress in Phrasal Verbs

CD 1 Track 22 A particle looks like a preposition, but it is part of a phrasal verb. When the verb and particle are separated, both the verb and particle are stressed. Listen to the examples.

EXAMPLES: Music always **cheers** me **up** when I'm sad.

We **worked** the problem **out** together.

Turn it **up**.

I **picked** it **out**.

A PRACTICE Listen and repeat these sentences with phrasal verbs. Mark the words that are stressed. Then listen and repeat.

1. It always cheers me up when I'm sad.

2. We worked the problem out together.

3. Turn it up.

4. I'll figure it out.

5. I picked it out.

6. Their music caught on.

7. I managed to get through the whole thing, but it took time.

B PRACTICE Now go back and mark the words that are stressed in the sentences with phrasal verbs from the Practice exercise on page 30. (Be sure the incorrect sentences are corrected.) Take turns reading them aloud with a partner.

Get Ready to Speak

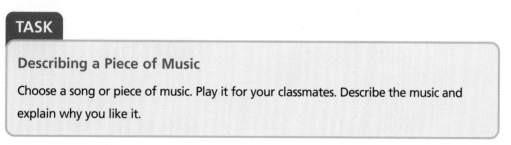

TASK

Describing a Piece of Music

Choose a song or piece of music. Play it for your classmates. Describe the music and explain why you like it.

1. Read the questions on the worksheet that follows. Then choose a song or piece of music to describe, and answer the questions about it.

Worksheet: My Favorite Music

1. What is the piece of music you chose?

_____

2. Describe the music.

_____

3. Why do you like it?

_____

4. What is your favorite part?

_____

5. How does it make you feel?

_____

6. Where and when do you listen to it?

_____

7. How often do you listen to it?

_____

8. How would you summarize this music's effect on you?

_____

9. What else do you want to say about it?

_____

2. Read your answers to the questions. Put your ideas in a logical order. Then describe your piece of music to a partner. Make changes as needed.

Remember to:

- use phrasal verbs.
- use correct stress.

Speak

Play your piece of music for your audience. Give your description of the music. When you have finished speaking, take questions from your audience.

WRITING

Read these topics. Choose one to write about.

1. Shaddox sees jazz as a source of optimism. Write about something that is a source of optimism for you.

2. Shaddox seems to include jazz in every part of her life. Is music important in your everyday life? Explain. Give at least two examples in your answer.

3. Write about the music you talked about in the Speaking section on pages 31–32. Explain how this music affects you.

4. Do you like jazz? Listen to some jazz. Describe it in your own words. Decide whether you like it or not. Give at least two reasons.

What do you believe?

As you listen to the essays in this book, think about your beliefs. Write your own *What I Believe* essay. Follow the steps on pages 132–135.

ALWAYS GO. . .
–Deirdre Sullivan

GETTING READY

 Listen and read about the essayist.

Meet Deirdre Sullivan

Deirdre Sullivan is a lawyer in Brooklyn, New York. Her job is to give people advice. But, in her personal life, she follows some advice her father gave her many years ago. He told Deirdre, or Dee as he called her, to attend the funerals of people she knew. For Sullivan, her father's advice has grown and changed into a life philosophy. She uses this belief in many different situations.

Connect to the Topic

Discuss these questions with a partner.

What is some valuable advice someone has given you? Do you still follow this advice today?

GLOSSARY

You will hear these words and expression in the essay. Read their definitions before you listen.

Funeral Terms

funeral /ˈfyunərəl/ *n.* ceremony, often religious, after someone dies

calling hours /ˈkɔlɪŋ aʊərz/ *n.* the time before a funeral when people visit the family of the person who died

sympathy /ˈsɪmpəθi/ *n.* feeling of support for someone who is sad, hurt, lonely, etc.

condolence line /kən ˈdoʊləns laɪn/ *n.* after a funeral, those who attended stand in a line and offer some words of sympathy to the family

Shiva call /ˈʃɪvə kɔl/ *n.* the Jewish tradition for calling hours

Expressing condolences

LISTENING

Listen for Main Ideas

CD 1 Track 24 Read these sentences. Then listen to Deirdre Sullivan's essay. Check (✓) the sentence that best summarizes the main idea.

☐ 1. Sullivan's personal philosophy of "always go to the funeral" means doing things for others when she has the time.

☐ 2. According to Sullivan, "always go to the funeral" means doing the right thing when she doesn't feel like it.

☐ 3. Sullivan thinks that people should always go to funerals because it helps people deal with the loss of their family member.

☐ 4. Sullivan believes going to funerals can teach kids a lot about life.

Vocabulary for Comprehension

CD 1 Track 26 Read and listen to these sentences. Then match the boldfaced words and expressions with their definitions on page 37.

_g_ 1. On the day of her math test, Mia pretended to be sick. She **got out of** taking the test.

____ 2. In his new high school, José felt uncomfortable in history class because he was still learning English. When his teacher asked him a question, he **stammered out** his answer in a quiet voice.

____ 3. When Jennifer wanted to stop piano lessons, her parents insisted she continue. They were **unequivocal**. Eventually, Jennifer was glad that her parents didn't let her give up.

____ 4. When Maxwell first became a surgeon, operating on people was stressful. However, today, performing operations is **a matter of course** for him.

____ 5. Sara feels her life in a small town is **humdrum**. She thinks life in a big city would be more exciting.

____ 6. Sometimes parents have a **battle** with their children over things like doing homework and cleaning their bedrooms.

____ 7. Bernard and his friends are excited about watching the game on Sunday. It's Italy **versus** Brazil.

____ 8. My friend looked **shell-shocked** after hanging up the telephone. I could tell something bad had happened.

____ 9. After his grandfather died and left him a large amount of money, James decided to **stick to** his original plan to attend medical school. Today he's a doctor.

____ 10. Mrs. Park gave Daniel a book of poems as **a gesture of kindness**. It wasn't his birthday. She just knew he would enjoy it.

_____ 11. When Fabian's older sister took him to her high school basketball game, it **meant the world to him**. He will never forget that day.

a. a way to show she cared   e. perfectly clear, definite   i. spoke brokenly

b. against   f. surprised and very upset   j. fight or struggle

c. routine, everyday   g. avoided   k. stay with

d. made him very happy   h. boring and ordinary

Listen for Details

A CD 1 Track 27 Read these sentences. Then listen to Sullivan's essay again. Write *T* (true) or *F* (false).

_____ 1. The first time Sullivan went to a funeral by herself she was sixteen.

_____ 2. There were other kids at Miss Emerson's funeral.

_____ 3. Sullivan was not able to say anything to Miss Emerson's parents.

_____ 4. Sullivan had been to five or six funerals by the time she was sixteen.

_____ 5. Her personal philosophy of going to funerals means getting in a car and going to calling hours of the funeral.

_____ 6. She makes small gestures of kindness because they can mean the world to others.

_____ 7. None of the people at her father's funeral were inconvenienced by attending it.

_____ 8. Sullivan was touched by the number of people who came to her father's funeral.

B CD 1 Track 28 Read these questions. Then listen to the essay again. Write your answers to the questions.

1. How did Sullivan feel as the only kid at Miss Emerson's funeral? Base your answer on her description.

_____

2. Sullivan gives three examples of doing the right thing when you don't really feel like it. What are these examples?

_____

3. What does Sullivan describe as "the most human, powerful, and humbling thing" she has ever seen?

_____

4. How does Sullivan probably feel today about having gone to Miss Emerson's funeral? Why do you think so?

_____

REACTING TO THE ESSAY

Discuss your answers to these questions.

1. Deirdre Sullivan describes seeing the people at her father's funeral by saying, "The memory of it still takes my breath away." Why do you think this was so important to her?
2. Sullivan says she believes in doing things that are perhaps inconvenient for her but mean a lot to others. What are some possible examples of this from daily life?
3. Do you agree with Sullivan? Do you believe it is important to do things that mean a lot to others but are only inconvenient for you? Explain.

BACKGROUND NOTES

Deirdre Sullivan lives and works in Brooklyn, New York. Brooklyn is located east of Manhattan's lowest point. Its population is approximately 2.5 million. Brooklyn is famous for its cultural diversity: the residents speak English, Spanish, Russian, French, Chinese, Yiddish, Italian, Polish, Hebrew, and Arabic in addition to other languages. People who live in Brooklyn enjoy its 19th–century architecture and many art galleries.

SPEAKING

In her essay, Deirdre Sullivan describes her personal philosophy of always going to funerals. For her, it means doing the right thing when she doesn't have to, and perhaps really doesn't want to. In this section, you will describe a time in the past when you did (or did not do) the right thing.

Build Fluency

Language: Expressing Satisfaction and Regret in the Past

Study the phrases for expressing satisfaction and regret in the past.

EXPRESSING SATISFACTION (YOU DID THE RIGHT THING.)	EXPRESSING REGRET (YOU DIDN'T DO THE RIGHT THING.)
I'm glad I did that.	**I wish I had** helped out. Next time I will.
It was the right thing to do.	**I should have** given him some money.
It felt good to do the right thing.	**It would have been a good idea to** send him a card.
I think she appreciated it.	**I know I could have** visited him, but I just didn't have the time.
It was a good thing to do.	**Why didn't I do that? I'm not sure. Maybe . . .**

PRACTICE Work with a partner. Read these situations. Complete the comments using two expressions from the chart. There may be more than one correct answer.

1. Yesterday, there was a man sitting outside the supermarket asking for money. I don't feel comfortable giving money to a stranger, so I bought him a sandwich instead. He smiled happily when I gave it to him.

   It felt good to buy that stranger lunch. I think he appreciated it.

2. My sister has to work late some nights, and when she does, her husband usually comes home early to make dinner for their children. My sister had to work late one night last week, and her husband was away on a business trip. I knew this, but I didn't do anything to help.

_____

_____

3. Last night I took the subway home around 9:00 P.M. I had worked all day long and was very tired. As I was going out of the subway station, I noticed an old woman having trouble going up the stairs. I looked at her, but didn't help her.

_____

_____

4. Last weekend there was a birthday party for a little boy who used to live next door. Now he lives with his family in another city. When his mother called and asked us to come to the party, I didn't say "yes" immediately. We already had plans to go to the beach. But after five minutes, I called her back and told her we could attend.

_____

_____

5. Last summer, my sister broke her leg. My father called to tell me the news one day after work. I was tired and wanted to stay home. When my father suggested I visit the hospital, I made some excuse and didn't go.

_____

_____

Pronunciation: Reductions with *Have*

CD 1 Track 29 In informal speech, we reduce helping verbs like **have**. In *should have*, *would have*, and *could have*, **have** sounds like [*uv*], or the word *of*. Listen to the examples.

EXAMPLES: should have /ʃədəv/

would have /wədəv/

I should have helped my neighbor. It would have meant a lot to him.

A PRACTICE Listen to the conversation. Then listen again and repeat.

A: Why didn't you study for your math test? You **could have** studied after the game.

B: I know—I **should have** studied. I was celebrating because my team won.

A: Well, it certainly **would have** been a good idea to study more and party less.

B PRACTICE Work with a partner. Take turns reading your answers to items 2, 3, and 5 in the Practice exercise on page 40. Reduce the verb *have* so that it sounds like *of*.

Get Ready to Speak

TASK

Describing Satisfaction and Regret for Past Actions

Describe a time in the past when you did (or did not do) the right thing. Explain the result and your feelings about it now.

1. Read the chart below. Then make notes about a time when you did (or didn't do) the right thing. Describe the situation. Explain what you did (or didn't do), the result, and your reaction. Then describe how you feel about it now.

	Example	Your ideas
Situation	*I lost contact with my good friend from high school for about 6 years.*	
What you did/didn't do	*I received an invitation to his wedding last summer, but didn't go.*	
Result	*He wrote me an e-mail asking me why I hadn't come.*	
Your reaction	*Felt bad— then decided to do the right thing—Responded to his e-mail—Invited him and his wife to my house for dinner—Gave them a wedding gift*	

How do you feel about that experience now? _____

_____

_____

2. Review your notes in the chart. Put your ideas in logical order. Work with a partner and practice describing the situation. Add interesting ideas or details. Take out information that is not important. Make changes as needed.

Remember to:

• express satisfaction or regret about your action. Use the expressions of satisfaction or regret on page 39.

• describe your feelings about it now.

• reduce *have* so it sounds like *of*.

Speak

Tell your story to a small group or to the class. When you have finished speaking, take questions from your audience.

WRITING

Read these topics. Choose one to write about.

1. Write about a time when you had to do something nice, but you didn't feel like it. What was the situation? Why didn't you feel like it? What was the outcome? You could also write about your topic from the Speaking section on pages 41–42.

2. Describe a time when someone did something that meant a lot to you. Explain why it was meaningful to you.

3. The first time Deirdre Sullivan went to calling hours by herself she was sixteen. Before going, she tried to get out of it, but her father insisted she go. Write the conversation between her and her father.

What do you believe?

As you listen to the essays in this book, think about your beliefs. Write your own *What I Believe* essay. Follow the steps on pages 132–135.

UNIT 5

THE MAKING OF POEMS
–Gregory Orr

GETTING READY

CD 1 Track 30 Listen and read about the essayist.

Meet Gregory Orr

Gregory Orr is a professor of English at the University of Virginia. When he was young, he caused a terrible accident. After that, he and his family felt shattered.[1] Orr's family had trouble talking to him. It made him feel numb.[2] He also felt completely alone. Reading and writing poems helped him feel alive.

---

[1] broken up into many small pieces
[2] unable to feel

Connect to the Topic

Discuss these questions with a partner.

• What kinds of things do you like to read?

• Do you like to talk about what you read with family and friends? Explain.

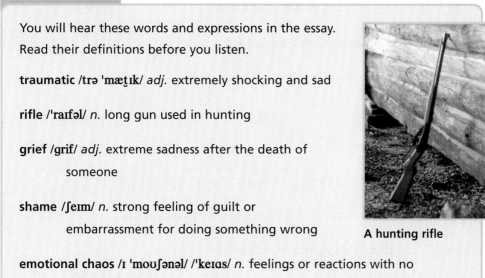

GLOSSARY

You will hear these words and expressions in the essay. Read their definitions before you listen.

traumatic /trə ˈmæt̬ɪk/ *adj.* extremely shocking and sad

rifle /ˈraɪfəl/ *n.* long gun used in hunting

grief /grif/ *adj.* extreme sadness after the death of someone

shame /ʃeɪm/ *n.* strong feeling of guilt or embarrassment for doing something wrong

A hunting rifle

emotional chaos /ɪ ˈmoʊʃənəl/ /ˈkeɪɑs/ *n.* feelings or reactions with no organization

LISTENING

Listen for Main Ideas

CD 1 Track 31 Read the question and answer choices. Then listen to Gregory Orr's essay. Circle the letter of the best answer to the question.

Why does Orr read and write poems?

    a. It helps him give meaning to his experiences.

    b. It helps him feel a connection to others.

    c. It helps him live and believe in living.

    d. All of the above.

Vocabulary for Comprehension

CD 1 Track 33 Read these words and their definitions. Then work in pairs. Use the words to complete the sentences below. Listen to the sentences to check your answers.

---

agonizing *adj.* extremely painful

live by *v.* follow as a guiding principle or belief

cut us off from *v.* isolated or separated us from

process *n.* method, order of doing something

process *v.* make sense of

transforming *v.* changing

proof *n.* evidence that shows something to be a fact

miracle *n.* something extraordinary and unexplainable by science

chaotic *adj.* completely disorganized, without order

triumph *n.* a victory

The hurricane that went through our area last year (1) _cut us off from_ the outside world for twenty-four hours. It was a scary experience. People reacted with strong emotions. They didn't know how to (2) _____ the loss of their houses. I could see how their lives had suddenly become (3) _____: they had no home and were unsure of where they would sleep that night. To help these people deal with the experience, everyone shared stories. This (4) _____ made them feel better.

One (5) _____ decision we had to make was leaving our dog behind. The helpers told us that a special animal group would pick up animals later.

The helpers worked hard and got us out of danger. As time passed and everyone helped to clean up, we watched the city as it was (6) _____ from a dirty, broken place to a clean, working one. The philosophy I now (7) _____ is the idea that we all must help our neighbors. Our experience is (8) _____ of how everyone's actions were a (9) _____ of human nature. What happened when we all worked together for the good of everyone was truly a (10) _____.

Listen for Details

A CD 1 Track 34 Read these sentences. Then listen to Orr's essay again. Complete the sentences with the words from the box.

connection	death	transforms	young
couldn't speak	proof	triumph	

1. When he was twelve, he was responsible for the _____ of a younger brother in a hunting accident.

2. After this tragedy, his family _____ to him about his brother's death.

3. He discovered poetry as a _____ person.

4. When he writes a poem, he _____ experience.

5. Even the saddest poem he writes is _____ he wants to survive.

6. Poems are a _____ over human isolation because they can be shared between poet and audience.

7. When he reads a poem he likes, he feels a _____ to the person who wrote it.

B CD 1 Track 35 Read these questions. Then listen to the essay again. Answer the questions.

1. What does Orr feel before and after making a poem?

   _____

2. Orr says, "As a young person, I found something to set against my growing sense of isolation and numbness: the making of poems." Which statement best summarizes this quote?

   a. I discovered something to fix my anger on: poetry.

   b. I found something to counterbalance my increasing feelings of being lonely: poetry.

   c. Poetry helped me understand other people better.

   d. Sharing poetry helped me to meet new people.

3. Why do other people's poems give Orr hope and courage?

   _____

   _____

REACTING TO THE ESSAY

Discuss your answers to these questions.

1. Orr describes making poems as giving him a feeling of "wild joy." Is there something that gives you a similar feeling? Explain.

2. Orr uses the word *miracle* to introduce the topic of sharing poems. What is a miracle? Do you agree that the sharing of a poem can be a miracle?

3. Orr believes that sharing poetry can help people process and understand confusing experiences in life. It also helps connect people and prevents isolation. What else can offer understanding and lessen human isolation?

CULTURE NOTES

The following is a poem written by Gregory Orr.

Father's Song

**Father
and daughter**

Yesterday, against admonishment,*
my daughter balanced on the couch back,
fell and cut her mouth.

Because I saw it happen I knew
she was not hurt, and yet
a child's blood so red
it stops a father's heart.

My daughter cried her tears;
I held some ice
against her lip.
That was the end of it.

Round and round: bow** *and kiss.*
I try to teach her caution;
she tried to teach me risk.

* warning
** bend

From *The Caged Owl: New and Selected Poems* by Gregory Orr.
Copyright © 2002 by Gregory Orr. Used by permission of Copper
Canyon Press. All rights reserved.

SPEAKING

In his essay, Gregory Orr talks about sharing poems. He believes that as audiences, or readers, we can also share different reactions to poems by talking about them. In this section, you will choose a poem and discuss its meaning in a group.

Build Fluency

Language: Participating in Small Groups

In a small group discussion, the responsibilities are shared. Group members take turns offering ideas to talk about, encouraging people to give more information, and summarizing what people have said. They use a mix of requests, general and specific questions, and statements to participate in the discussion.

EXPRESSIONS FOR PARTICIPATING IN SMALL GROUPS		
Beginning Discussions	**Getting More Information**	**Summarizing**
(Bob), what do you think?	Good point. Could you tell us a little more?	As (Anna) said, this poem is _____.
Tell me your impressions of the poem.	Can you explain why?	To summarize what (Martin) said, _____.
	Why do you think the writer used those words?	In summary, (we) _____.
What does the poem mean to you?	Can you give an example?	
	(Luis), do you agree with that?	

PRACTICE Work with a partner. Match the question or statement to its discussion situation. More than one correct answer is possible.

Question or Statement

_____ 1. Can you give an example of what you mean?

_____ 2. Well, what do you think?

_____ 3. In summary, it looks like we all agree.

_____ 4. Could you tell us more?

Situation

a. The speaker is summarizing another's opinion.

b. The speaker has just finished reading a poem and is beginning the discussion.

c. The speaker is asking for more information by asking for an example.

d. The speaker is keeping the discussion going.

_____ 5. As Anna said, it's very
interesting and something
we have all experienced.

e. The speaker is making a final
summary and ending the
discussion.

_____ 6. Tell me your first impressions.

f. The speaker could be starting the
discussion, or keeping it going.

Pronunciation: Word Stress

CD 1 Track 36 Stress content words when reading poems aloud. Content words
include nouns, verbs, adjectives, and adverbs. Read your poem selections aloud to
each other. Stress the content words and give less volume to the other words.
Listen to the example.

EXAMPLE:

Sun on snow covering the ground

like a blanket for miles around—

I prepare for spring.

A PRACTICE Listen to the example again. This time repeat, line by line.

B PRACTICE Read and listen to the discussion. Then work with two other
students and read it aloud. Use correct stress.

A: Tell me your impressions of the poem.

B: In my opinion, it's a poem about loving nature.

C: Yes. I agree. It says everything in life comes from nature.

A: Can you give an example of what you mean?

C: Well, I mean plants, light—even a smile comes from nature.

Get Ready to Speak

TASK

Discussing the Meaning of a Poem

Choose a poem, or write one, and discuss its meaning with your group.

1. Haiku is a form of Japanese poetry about nature and the seasons. Each poem has three lines. Read the haiku poem. Then read the notes about the poem.

> Sun on snow covering the ground
> like a blanket for miles around—
> I prepare for spring.

poem's main message	poem's connection to daily life	one phrase I like and why	poem's connection to me
-renewal of life -cycle of life	-see nature every day -take time to look at it -continually grows and renews	*Sun on snow;* -sun gives heat to renew -snow can protect -Sun's heat and protection = new life in spring	-My childhood = grew up in a place with a lot of snow -Always love spring — like a reward for putting up with cold winter

2. Choose a short poem or haiku you like, or write one. Make notes that answer the following questions about the poem, as the notes above do.

   • What is the main message of the poem?

   • What is one phrase that you particularly like? Why?

   • What is the poem's connection to daily life and to your life?

3. Review your notes about your poem. Write three or four questions or statements to facilitate a group discussion. Then work in a small group and practice presenting your poem. Make changes as needed.

Remember to:

- describe the poem's main message.
- give one phrase that you particularly like and explain why.
- explain the poem's connection to daily life and to your life.
- use appropriate word stress.
- use a variety of expressions from the chart in the Build Fluency section on page 50 to aid discussion. Use requests, questions, and statements to facilitate discussion of your poem.

Speak

Change groups. Present your poem. Then have a group discussion of your poem. Help the other members of your group participate in the discussion. Then summarize the discussion.

WRITING

Read these topics. Choose one to write about.

1. Describe something you have read that has had an important impact on you. Explain why it was important to you.

2. Paraphrase the meaning of the poem you chose in the Speaking section on pages 52–53. Cite one line or phrase you especially like. Give reasons why you like it.

3. Do you agree with Orr's description of the power of poetry? Do you even like poetry? Explain. Use an example of a poem if you have one.

What do you believe?

As you listen to the essays in this book, think about your beliefs. Write your own *What I Believe* essay. Follow the steps on pages 132–135.

UNIT 6

WHEN ORDINARY PEOPLE ACHIEVE EXTRAORDINARY THINGS
–Jody Williams

GETTING READY

CD 1 Track 37 Listen and read about the essayist.

> ### Meet Jody Williams
>
> Jody Williams is the head of the International Campaign to Ban[1] Landmines. The organization works to ban the production of landmines, which are small bombs hidden in the ground that explode when someone walks or drives over them. As a young person, Williams never expected to work to solve global problems. But when two people asked her to organize the landmine campaign, she accepted the challenge. Since then, she has worked with ordinary people all over the world to do extraordinary things. Together, they are finding solutions to the global landmine problem.

[1]stop or eliminate

Connect to the Topic

Discuss these questions with a partner.

- Landmines are a global problem. What do you know about landmines?
- What are they?
- Where are they common?
- Why are they a problem?

GLOSSARY

You will hear these words and expressions in the essay. Read their definitions before you listen.

campaign /kæm ˈpeɪn/ *n.* a series of planned activities to reach a specific goal

activist /ˈæktəvɪst/ *n.* a person who fights for a specific cause or change

defending /dɪ ˈfɛndɪŋ/ *v.* protecting someone or something from being attacked

power /ˈpaʊɚ/ *n.* ability or strength

voice (one's) opinion /vɔɪs wʌnz əˈpɪnyən/ *exp.* speak or express one's ideas publicly

taking action /teɪkɪŋ ˈækʃən/ *v.* doing something specific to solve a problem

Partially covered landmine lying on the ground

LISTENING

Listen for Main Ideas

CD 1 Track 38 Read these sentences. Then listen to Jody Williams's essay. Write *T* (true) or *F* (false).

_____ 1. Williams believes that the difference between an ordinary person and an extraordinary person depends on his or her job title or position.

_____ 2. It was Williams's idea to start the landmine campaign.

_____ 3. Williams cares what people say about her.

_____ 4. Williams believes that the only thing that changes the world is taking action.

Vocabulary for Comprehension

CD 1 Track 40 Read and listen to a conversation about a brochure on landmines. Then match the boldfaced words and expressions with their definitions on page 57.

A: Let's talk about what ideas to include in the brochure. What can we say that will encourage people to demand that governments **confront** the problem?

B: Well, first we need to get the attention of people who aren't affected directly by the violence. We want them to care. This is difficult because our culture **glorifies** violence.

A: Yes, that's true. Perhaps we can start with the personal story of a landmine survivor . . .

C: That sounds good, but we should be positive and suggest ways to **seek solutions** to the problem, too.

A: I agree. We need to offer real ways people can help.

B: That's right. But it still takes **courage** for people to take action. People don't believe they can really help.

A: Yes, that's a big **challenge**. Ordinary people often feel that what they do is **irrelevant**. We need to change that belief.

C: Let's say something like, "Working together we can **accomplish** extraordinary things."

A: That sounds great. Let's also say, "Taking action is your **right**." We all have the right to live in a less violent world. It's also your **responsibility**. Each of us must work to help the victims of violence.

B: Let's add, "Don't just talk about it. **Back up** your words with action!"

A: Let's start writing all of this down!

1. _____*irrelevant*_____ unimportant, not mattering

2. _____ offer support

3. _____ duty or obligation to take care of something or someone

4. _____ succeed in doing something

5. _____ deal with something very difficult or bad

6. _____ difficult task that tests your skills in an interesting way

7. _____ bravery

8. _____ something you have or are allowed to do according to the law

9. _____ look for answers; try to find answers

10. _____ makes something look or seem much better than it is

Listen for Details

A CD 1 Track 41 Read these sentences. Then listen to Williams's essay again. Circle the letter of the answer that best completes each sentence.

1. According to Jody Williams, extraordinary people _____.

    a. do things to improve life for all of us

    b. only work in global activism

    c. work for the government

    d. have important jobs

2. When Williams and two others began the campaign in Washington, D.C., she _____.

    a. didn't know how to start

    b. didn't know much about landmines

    c. had several ideas about how to start it

    d. knew the campaign would be successful

3. According to Williams, the campaign is about landmines and about people _____.

    a. working with governments in a different way

    b. making friends around the world

    c. taking power away from governments

    d. working alone to change the world

4. According to Williams, an example of being courageous, or brave, means daring to _____.

    a. lead

    b. glorify violence and war

    c. voice your opinion

    d. believe in the world

5. Williams would most likely say _____.

   a. "I have to do my best on good days and bad days."

   b. "I try to do the right thing, even if people don't notice."

   c. "I do the right thing only when people are looking."

   d. "I've got to do things the right way so I can be popular."

6. According to Williams, we can accomplish extraordinary things if enough ordinary people _____.

   a. decide to become extraordinary

   b. stop trying to be popular

   c. act on their desire for a better world

   d. dream about a better world

B **CD 1 Track 42** Read these sentences. Then listen to the essay again. Check (✓) the sentences Williams would agree with.

☐ 1. I have power because I am an individual.

☐ 2. Results are seen in what people do, not what they say.

☐ 3. It can take courage to get information from a lot of different places.

☐ 4. If enough people worry about global problems, the problems will be solved.

REACTING TO THE ESSAY

Discuss your answers to these questions.

1. Williams says, "I believe words are easy. I believe the truth is told in the actions we take." What does she mean by this? Do you agree? Explain.

2. What do you think motivated Williams to become a global activist?

3. Would you like a job like Williams's? Explain.

Jody Williams discusses working to solve the landmine problem in her essay. Read these facts about landmines.

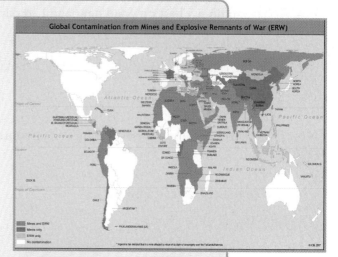

Map of landmine problems in the world

- The United Nations estimates that there are 110 million landmines in over 70 countries. About 100 million of them are too small to be seen by ordinary people.

- Landmines kill and wound over 20,000 people every year.

- Twelve countries hold 50 percent of the landmines in the world and have the largest casualties: Afghanistan, Angola, Bosnia-Herzegovina, Cambodia, Croatia, Eritrea, Iraq, Mozambique, Namibia, Nicaragua, Somalia, and Sudan.

- There are many de-mining (clean-up) programs. For example, land that was cleaned it mines was donated to the people who cleaned it up.

SPEAKING

In her essay, Williams states her belief that the only way to change the world is to take action and not to wait for others to solve problems. She believes that ordinary people must work together to make the world a better place. In this section, you will identify a local or global problem and discuss ways to solve it. Then you will present the results of this discussion.

Build Fluency

Language: Keeping a Discussion Going

The way you respond to ideas can keep a discussion going. There are many ways to respond. Study the common expressions in the chart.

KEEPING A CONVERSATION GOING	
Stating an opinion	**Example:** We really should. . .
Asking for more information	**Examples:** How so? Why do you say that?
Expressing surprise	**Examples:** Really? That's a surprise. Do you really think so? Wow! I didn't know that. Are you serious? (strong)
Expressing doubt	**Examples:** Are you sure about that? Well, I don't know about that. I'm not (so) convinced.
Agreeing (reluctantly) with someone	**Examples:** Well, I suppose you're right. I guess you have a point there.

PRACTICE Write a conversation using the expressions from the chart above. Follow the directions in parentheses.

1. A: (State your opinion about pollution levels in your city.)

   _____

2. B: (Respond and express surprise.)

   _____

3. A: (Give reasons for the need to reduce the amount of pollution.)

   _____

4. B: (Ask for more information.)

   _____

5. A: (Provide an example of something people can do to help.)

_____

6. B: (Agree and add your own comment.)

_____

7. A: (Suggest another thing people can do to help.)

_____

8. B: (Express doubt about this.)

_____

9. A: (Give a reason to convince person B.)

_____

10. B: (Agree reluctantly.)

_____

Pronunciation: Intonation for Surprise and Doubt

CD 1 Track 43 Use rising intonation and a louder voice to express surprise. This is true when you use a question to respond to others' ideas with surprise. Listen to the examples.

EXAMPLES: A: We just opened a local office for the Landmine Campaign.

        B: **Really?** Ours opened just six months ago. Let's get together and talk.

        C: **Are you serious?** We want to open one, too. Tell me how you did it!

Use falling intonation and say words slowly to express doubt.

EXAMPLES: A: I believe people should stop using clothes dryers.

        B: **I don't know.** I'm not sure it would really save enough energy to improve the situation.

        C: **Well**, it takes longer to do the laundry like that, **but I suppose you're right**. Reducing energy use always helps.

A [CD 1 Track 43] **PRACTICE** Listen to these sentences. Check (✓) if the speakers are surprised, doubtful, or something else (Other). Then practice saying the sentences with the proper intonation.

"Well, lowering energy use at home might help, but it's factories that cause the biggest part of the problem."

	Surprise	Doubt	Other
1. I'm not so convinced.	☐	☐	☐
2. I know. It makes me very angry.	☐	☐	☐
3. Wow! I didn't know that.	☐	☐	☐

B Go back to the Practice exercise on pages 61–62. Practice your conversation with a partner. Use correct intonation to express surprise and doubt.

Get Ready to Speak

TASK

Inviting Others to Agree and Comment

Identify a local or global problem. Offer suggestions about how people can take action to help solve it. In groups, list your ideas and invite others to agree with you and comment.

1. Make a list of three global or local problems. Think of two ways people can take action to improve each problem. Note these actions in your chart.

	Global or Local Problem	**How can people take action?**
a.		

b.	
c.	

2. Work in groups. Choose one problem to talk about. Describe the problem and state your belief about it. Offer solutions or ways to take action. Practice speaking about the problem. Make changes as needed.

Remember to:

- use the phrases for responding to their ideas while other group members are speaking.

- use correct intonation to express surprise or doubt.

Speak

Present your problem and solutions to a different group. Take questions and comments from your audience during your presentation.

WRITING

Read these topics. Choose one to write about.

1. Write about your topic from the Speaking section on pages 63–64. Explain two practical strategies people can use to help solve the problem.

2. Think of some other global activism campaigns, such as Greenpeace and Doctors Without Borders. Describe the work the organization does and why.

3. Write about an ordinary person whom you think is extraordinary. Explain why you think so. Give examples.

What do you believe?

As you listen to the essays in this book, think about your beliefs. Write your own *What I Believe* essay. Follow the steps on pages 132–135.

DISRUPTING MY COMFORT ZONE
–Brian Grazer

GETTING READY

CD 2 Track 2 Listen and read about the essayist.

> ### Meet Brian Grazer
>
> Brian Grazer is a successful Hollywood movie and television producer. He has won a lot of awards for his work. In his personal and professional life, Grazer likes a challenge. He likes to disrupt his comfort zone by trying new things, like surfing and meeting interesting people. Grazer's belief keeps him looking for new challenges all the time.

Connect to the Topic

Discuss these questions with a partner.

Grazer believes that trying new and challenging things helps to "keep him in the game." What are the advantages and disadvantages of trying new and challenging things? Write two ideas in each column.

Advantages

1.

2.

Disadvantages

1.

2.

GLOSSARY

You will hear these words and expressions in the essay. Read their definitions before you listen.

Professions

trial lawyers traɪəl lɔyəz/ *n.* people whose job it is to defend people in legal courts, also **attorneys**

neurosurgeons /ˈnʊroʊ ˈsəˈdʒənz/ *n.* medical doctors who treat and operate on the brain and nervous system

CIA agents /si aɪ eɪ ˈeɪdʒənts/ *n.* people who work for the Central Intelligence Agency, part of U.S. law enforcement

embryologists /ˌɛmbri ˈalədʒɪsts/ *n.* scientists who study embryos, or early life before birth

fire walkers /faɪə ωɔkəz/ *n.* people who walk on burning wood or coals

hypnotists /ˈhɪpnətɪsts/ *n.* people who can make other people relax deeply enough to access the part of the mind that has thoughts and feelings they often don't realize they have

Hypnotist with client in deep relaxation

> **forensic anthropologists** /fə'rɛnsɪk ænθrə 'pɑlədʒɪsts/ *n.* scientists who investigate bones (skeletons) at a crime scene and report their findings to a legal court
>
> **physicists** /fɪzəsɪsts/ *n.* scientists who study physical objects and natural forces such as light, heat, and movement
>
> **biologists** /baɪ 'ɑlədʒɪsts/ *n.* scientists who study natural life and living things

LISTENING

Listen for Main Ideas

CD 2 Track 3 Read these sentences. Then listen to Brian Grazer's essay. Circle the letter of the sentence that best summarizes his main message.

a. Disrupting my comfort zone is good for my professional life, but I try to avoid physical or mental challenge if it's too difficult.

b. Challenging myself means I will be disappointed; this makes me try harder to be successful.

c. Challenging myself with people, work, or activities helps me grow and learn.

d. Meeting and talking with experts and famous people gives me all my ideas about how to succeed in my work.

Vocabulary for Comprehension

CD 2 Track 5 Read and listen to the interview. Then match the boldfaced words and expressions with their definitions on pages 69–70.

A: I'm here with Mira Shona, a competitive surfer and mother of two children. Hi, Mira. What do you enjoy most about surfing?

B: Well, it really shakes me up. It challenges me, so I never get bored.

A: What's the hardest part?

B: It's when I have to go to a two-day surfing competition, and my children ask me to stay home with them. They actually (1) **beg me** not to go. I have to do lots of convincing and lots of (2) **cajoling**, usually with ice cream.

A: Has anyone ever questioned you about your lifestyle choice?

B: Yes, people have criticized me for my choice, but never laughed at me or (3) **ridiculed** me. I think many people don't (4) **have a taste for** an exciting life. People avoid challenges and prefer routine.

A: What's one advantage of being a mother who surfs?

B: Well, the other surfers keep me young. I always hear about new music and TV shows. I know what's happening in (5) **pop culture**.

A: Where do you get the energy to train and raise two children?

B: I don't know! I often wonder why I (6) **subject** myself **to** the physical demands, but I love being an athlete and a mother. It's what I do. It's important to find a balance and (7) **avoid** becoming exhausted. I get lots of sleep every night.

A: And speaking of your children, is that a (8) **tattoo** of them on your arm?

B: Yes, it is. A friend of mine is an artist and designed it for me.

A: Finally, You've written a book about your life philosophy. Can you (9) **paraphrase** that philosophy for us?

B: Challenging myself makes me feel awake and alive. It (10) **keeps me in the game**!

___8___ a. a picture or message permanently marked on your skin with a needle and ink

_____ b. music, movies, and products that are familiar to most people in the society

_____ c. persuading someone to do something by repeated asking, being nice, or promising

_____ d. laughed at someone or something when you think he, she, or it is stupid

_____ e. ask for something in an anxious or urgent way

_____ f. like something and appreciate it

_____ g. not do something because it's bad or you don't like it

_____ h. say what someone has said in a shorter or clearer way

_____ i. helps a person stay competitive in a sport or in life

_____ j. force someone or something to experience something very bad or difficult

CULTURE NOTES

Brian Grazer talks about learning to surf in his essay. Read the definitions for the words related to his surfing experience.

swells /swɛlz/ n. large amounts of ocean water built up just before becoming waves

tattoo /tæˈtu/ n. permanent picture drawn on a person's skin with a needle and ink

terror /tɛrɚ/ n. extreme fear

R.I.P. /ɚ. aɪ. pi./ *abbr.* "Rest in Peace," sometimes seen on a tattoo but most commonly seen on a headstone in a cemetery

In his essay, Brian Grazer talks about meeting with some well-known people. Read about them.

Carlos Castaneda (1931–1991), Peruvian writer whose books became popular in the 1960s

Jonas Salk (1914–1995), American physician and researcher, famous for the development of the first polio vaccine

Fidel Castro (1926–), President of Cuba from 1976 to 2008

Listen for Details

A CD 2 Track 6 Read these sentences. Then listen to Grazer's essay again. Write *T* (true) or *F* (false). Then correct the false sentences.

_____ 1. Grazer was afraid when he went surfing on Oahu.

_____ 2. Grazer enjoys creating daily challenges for himself.

_____ 3. Grazer thought the people on his list could give him work.

_____ 4. Each expert he met treated him with respect.

_____ 5. Grazer learned something from Edward Teller.

_____ 6. In thirteen years, Grazer has made more than twenty movies and fifty TV shows.

_____ 7. Grazer meets with challenging people because a biologist told him it was fun.

_____ 8. What Grazer likes about learning to surf is the challenge, discomfort, and uncertainty.

B CD 2 Track 7 Read these sentences. Then listen to the essay again. Circle the letter of the sentence or phrase that best completes each sentence.

1. Grazer met with experts and famous people _____.

   a. to be successful at his job

   b. to keep growing

   c. for the fun of it

   d. for a documentary film

2. Grazer would most likely say that _____.

   a. life is difficult, so we should not make it harder than it is

   b. in the entertainment business it's always good to feel uncomfortable

   c. finding new things to do every day makes him happy

   d. having a routine is the secret to success

3. An example of disrupting Grazer's comfort zone might be _____.

   a. having a meeting with his production staff

   b. interviewing this year's world surfing champion

   c. doing the grocery shopping

   d. spending time with his family and friends

REACTING TO THE ESSAY

Discuss your answers to these questions.

1. Look back at the Connect to the Topic section on page 67. Can you add new advantages or disadvantages? After listening to this essay, has your opinion about doing new and challenging things changed? Explain.

2. Grazer likes to meet with people he thinks can teach him something. What important person or expert would you most like to meet? Why?

3. Grazer says a biologist he once met said, "If you're not growing, you're dying," Do you agree? How do you see yourself growing? Explain.

SPEAKING

In his essay, Brian Grazer states his belief in challenging himself all the time. He says this keeps him in the game. In this section, you will present a list of five ways we can challenge ourselves.

Build Fluency

Language: Using *Recommend* and *Suggest*

Use the verbs *recommend* and *suggest* to offer your ideas and make suggestions. Read the chart. Note the forms that follow *recommend* and *suggest*.

MAKING SUGGESTIONS WITH *RECOMMEND* AND *SUGGEST*

• After *recommend* and *suggest*, use *that* + (new) subject + the base form of the verb.	**Examples:** base form • I **suggest** that you **learn** a new sport. • John's doctor **recommends** that he **play** tennis.
• If the subject is the same, use the *-ing* form of the verb after *recommend* and *suggest*.	**Examples:** *-ing* form • Jane **recommends going** to Prague on our trip • Kamala **suggests trying** a new sport.

PRACTICE Read these situations. Make recommendations and suggestions. Use the words in parentheses. Write complete sentences.

1. A: I feel like I don't have much energy.

    B: *I recommend exercising more often* .

    (recommend / exercise often)

2. A: My sister is looking for an interesting study abroad program.

    B: _____ .

    (suggest that / study in Asia)

3. A: I'm always bored on the weekends.

    B: _____ .

    (recommend / biking)

4. A: Did you know that my friend and I both love outdoor sports?

    B: _____
    _____ .

    (suggest that / learn to rock climb together)

5. A: Joan has always wanted to sing in public and she has a great voice.

    B: _____
    _____ .

    (recommend that / sing / at our local bar on Friday night)

6. A: I'm a pretty good golfer, and have played golf as a hobby for many years, but I'd like a new challenge.

   B: _____ .

   (suggest / entering a competition)

Pronunciation: Unstressed *Schwa*

CD 2 Track 8 In words with two or more syllables, one syllable is often unstressed.[1] It is pronounced with a reduced vowel sound called **schwa** (/ə/) Listen to the examples.

EXAMPLES: *ago   today   recommend   suggest*

The following reduced verbs with *go* are also pronounced with a schwa.

> I have to go.
>
> I want to go.
>
> I'm going to go.

A PRACTICE Listen to the conversation. Underline the unstressed syllables pronounced with the schwa sound. Then work with a partner. Discuss your answers and practice the conversation.

A: I just got a new surfboard.

B: Really? I bought my surfboard two years ago. Do you know what you have to do to keep it in good condition? Can I make a recommendation?

A: Sure.

B: Make sure you wash off the saltwater after each time you use it.

A: Thanks. Do you want to go surfing?

B: Absolutely! I'm going to go get my board now.

---

[1]Exceptions include words with prefixes such as *preview, rewind, debug* where *pre-, re-,* and *de-* are all pronounced with a tense /i/ vowel.

B PRACTICE Go back to the Practice exercise on pages 73–74. Work with a partner and take turns reading the statements and expressions. Focus on the unstressed schwa sound.

Get Ready to Speak

TASK

Making Recommendations

Create and present a list of five ways we can challenge ourselves in life, work, or study. Make recommendations to your classmates.

1. Brainstorm ideas about creating challenges in life. Work with a partner. Partner A: Choose a word from the list below. Say it out loud. Partner B: Say the first thing that comes into your mind when you hear that word. Write it down. Continue with all of the words. Then switch roles.

   sports _____   communication _____

   cooking _____   study   _____

   friendship _____   work   _____

                                          (your idea)   _____

2. Review the words you thought of in exercise 1. Create a list of five suggestions for ways people can challenge themselves. Give at least one example for five of the words on your list. Work with a partner and practice presenting your list of suggestions. Make changes as needed.

   Remember to:
   • use complete sentences with *recommend* and *suggest*.
   • use a schwa sound for appropriate unstressed vowels.

Speak

Give your presentation. When you have finished speaking, take questions from your audience.

WRITING

Read these topics. Choose one to write about.

1. Write about one of your ideas from the list you created in the Speaking section on page 75. Why is it important? How does it challenge people?

2. Refer to question 2 in the Reacting to the Essay section on page 72. Write about a famous person or an expert you'd like to meet. Explain who the person is and why you would like to meet him or her. Then write a list of questions you would ask that person.

3. Grazer says that many people avoid physical and mental challenge. Do you think people would be happier if they didn't try to avoid these things? Explain.

4. How do you disrupt your comfort zone? Write about what you do that keeps you feeling alive and "in the game."

What do you believe?

As you listen to the essays in this book, think about your beliefs. Write your own *What I Believe* essay. Follow the steps on pages 132–135.

A GOAL OF SERVICE TO HUMANKIND
–Anthony Fauci

GETTING READY

CD 2 Track 9 Listen and read about the essayist.

Meet Anthony Fauci

Anthony Fauci is a physician and medical researcher. His research focuses on diseases such as HIV/AIDS. He organizes his life around three guiding principles.[1] These principles keep Fauci anchored[2] and focused. They also help him stay humble so that he focuses on the work rather than on himself or his success. His goal is to serve humankind through his work.

[1] personal rules people live by every day

[2] in one place

Connect to the Topic

Discuss these questions with a partner.

Anthony Fauci's beliefs have helped him become successful. Think about someone you admire and think is successful.

- Why do you admire this person?
- In what way is this person a success?
- What guiding principles do you think he or she follows?

GLOSSARY

You will hear these words and expressions in the essay. Read their definitions before you listen.

public service /ˈpʌblɪk sɚvɪs/ *n.* work in governmental institutions that helps a country's citizens

infectious diseases /ɪnˈfɛkʃəs dɪzˈɪzɪz/ *n.* sicknesses that transfer from one person to another

alleviate /əˈlivi,eɪt/ *v.* make something less bad; give relief

make an impact on /meɪk ən ˈɪmpækt ɔn/ *exp.* have a strong effect on someone or something; more commonly: **have an impact on**

physician /fɪ ˈzɪʃən/ *n.* medical doctor

public health catastrophe /pʌblɪk hɛlθ kəˈtæstrəfi/ *n.* diseases or events that affect such a large number of people that governments must help

LISTENING

Listen for Main Ideas

CD 2 Track 10 Read these questions. Then listen to Anthony Fauci's essay. Circle the letter of the phrase that best answers each question.

1. What is Fauci's first guiding principle?

   a. always search for knowledge

   b. always experiment

   c. always read scientific journals

   d. never get bored

2. What is Fauci's second guiding principle?

   a. worrying a lot

   b. apologizing for his excellence

   c. being a perfectionist

   d. sweating as much as he can

3. What is Fauci's third guiding principle?

   a. believing in his goals

   b. finding the answers to HIV/AIDS

   c. believing in himself

   d. serving humankind

Vocabulary for Comprehension

CD 2 Track 12 Read and listen to the letter. Then match the boldfaced words and expressions with their definitions.

Hi Allison,

How are you? Sorry for taking so long to respond. I've also had a lot of exams this week.

It sounds like you're having a difficult time. I understand. We're always (1) **striving** to do our best in class, on exams, and with patients. There's little time to relax. And there's so much pressure to be successful. We have to be (2) **perfectionists**. I know I'm not perfect!

Of course, school and work cause us (3) **anxiety**. We're always thinking and running from place to place. Anxiety can leave you with the (4) **nagging** feeling that you're forgetting something. We need time to relax.

I'm sorry to hear your boss criticized you. The same thing happened to me. Why do bosses want us to have a feeling of (5) **inadequacy**? You know you're smart and capable. Don't let him make you think differently.

We're both doing very well! We have only one year of medical school left. We have the (6) **potential** to do great things.

Our desire to be doctors and help people (7) **drives** us. If we stay (8) **focused on** our goals, we will get there. You have a real (9) **thirst** for knowledge. You're probably just working too hard. Remember to take time to relax. As they say, (10) "**Don't sweat the small stuff**!" Just get some sleep.

Good luck on your exams!

Nina

_____ a. thinking clearly about

_____ b. people who try to do everything in exactly the right way

_____ c. tension, worry

_1_ d. working very hard all the time

_____ e. worry about things that are not important

_____ f. constantly bothering or bugging someone

_____ g. motivates or pushes

_____ h. not being good enough

_____ i. desire or want of something

_____ j. possibility

Listen for Details

A CD 2 Track 13 Read these sentences. Then listen to Fauci's essay again. Circle the letter of the phrase that best completes each sentence.

1. Fauci believes he has a personal responsibility to _____.

   a. persuade people to join him in his quest

   b. package information

   c. improve people's lives

   d. challenge society

2. Fauci considers his job _____.

   a. an anchor in his life

   b. a heavy burden

   c. a gift

   d. an easy one

3. Fauci rarely gets bored because he _____.

   a. does his own research

   b. is always learning new things

   c. goes to the lab every other day

   d. tries to see patients as much as possible

4. As a perfectionist, Fauci has a lot of anxiety. This anxiety _____.

    a. creates an unhealthy tension

    b. leaves him without a purpose

    c. makes him feel powerless

    d. drives him to do his best

5. Through most of his professional life, he has _____.

    a. been misguided

    b. focused on the HIV/AIDS crisis

    c. trained other physicians

    d. tried to improve his potential

B **CD 2 Track 14** In his essay, Fauci gives examples of his three guiding principles. Read the examples below. Then listen to the essay again. Check (✓) the correct principle for each example.

Examples	Principles		
	Thirst for knowledge	Strive for excellence	Serve humankind
1. doing an experiment in the lab			
2. knowing society is more important than he is			
3. being committed to confronting the HIV/AIDS crisis			
4. constantly trying to improve himself			
5. taking care of a patient			

REACTING TO THE ESSAY

Discuss your answers to these questions.

1. According to Fauci, his anxiety has a purpose: It drives him to try to be perfect. Do you agree with Fauci that this is a good quality in a medical doctor and scientist? Explain.

2. Fauci says he considers himself a perpetual student. In what other professions is it necessary to be learning all the time?

3. Which of the following makes life easiest? Explain.

   a. worrying only about big things

   b. worrying only about small things

   c. worrying about both big and small things

BACKGROUND NOTES

Anthony Fauci talks about his guiding principles as they relate to his job. Fauci works for the National Institutes of Health (NIH), which is part of the U.S. Department of Health and Human Services. The NIH is a medical research organization, funded by the government. NIH doctors advise the U.S. government on how best to treat medical conditions. Dr. Fauci is director of the National Institute of Allergy and Infectious Diseases.

A scientist in a protective suit conducts research in a lab

SPEAKING

In his essay, Anthony Fauci identifies the three principles that guide his life. In this section, you will give a short speech about one of your guiding principles.

Build Fluency

Language: Signposting

To organize information in a speech, use signposting language. Signposting helps listeners know when you are moving from one section to the next, or from a main idea to an example.

SIGNPOSTING LANGUAGE	
Introduction	**Examples:** • **Good morning/afternoon/evening.** • **My name is** _____ **and I work/study** at _____. • **I'd like to talk to you about** a guiding principle in my life/study/work: _____.
Identifying your main idea	**Examples:** • **One principle I use** in my life/study/work **is . . .** • **I believe in** (+ gerund) I believe in _striving_ for excellence.
Giving an example	**Examples:** • **This is important to me because . . .** • **For example, . . .** • **I use this principle when . . .**
Explaining the result	**Example:** • **As a result, . . .**
Concluding	**Examples:** • **In conclusion, . . .** • **To sum up, . . .**
Closing the speech	**Examples:** • **Thank you for your attention.** • **Are there any questions?**

PRACTICE The following sentences make a short speech. Read the sentences and put them in order. Number them from 1–7. Then decide which section of the speech each sentence belongs in.

Speech Sentences   Section of the Speech

_____ a. I believe in having a thirst for knowledge.   _____

_____ b. Thank you for listening.   _____

__1__ c. Good morning.   *introduction*

_____ d. In conclusion, having a thirst for
         knowledge helps me be a better doctor.   _____

_____ e. I'd like to talk to you about a guiding
         principle in my work.   _____

_____ f. As a result, they begin to trust me sooner.   _____

_____ g. For example, I've learned to listen more
         closely to my patients when they explain
         things to me.   _____

Pronunciation: Pauses with Signposting Language

CD 2 Track 15 Use short pauses after these signposting expressions. Pauses help your listeners follow your ideas. Listen to the examples.

Good morning.	Good afternoon.	Good evening.
For example,	As a result,	In conclusion,
To sum up,	Are there any questions?	However,

EXAMPLE: In conclusion, (pause) I believe working hard for what you believe in
            will always bring you closer to your goals.

A CD 2 Track 15 PRACTICE Listen to the short speech. Listen for the signposting expressions. Write *P* where you hear a pause.

Living in a Foreign Country

Good morning. My name is Mario, and I work for a computer company. Last year, I was transferred from Milan, Italy, to Amsterdam in the Netherlands. Today I'd like to talk to you about one principle that has helped me live in a foreign country: being open to new experiences. I believe in being open to new experiences. Living in a different country means I sometimes must make changes to my lifestyle. For example, I'm used to taking my time and eating pasta at lunchtime. However, in the Netherlands most people just eat a sandwich and go right back to work. The whole lunch break takes about 35 minutes! Instead of eating pasta at lunch, I now eat a sandwich. As a result, I get more work done during the day, and I have more time for friends in the evening.

In conclusion, being open to new experiences has helped me live more comfortably in a foreign country.

Thank you for your attention. Are there any questions?

B PRACTICE Go back to the Practice exercise on page 85. On a separate piece of paper, write the sentences in the correct order. Work with a partner and read the speech out loud. Practice using brief pauses that last about one second. Your pace should give listeners enough time to take brief notes.

Get Ready to Speak

TASK

Giving a Speech

Give a short speech about one guiding principle that you live by. Include examples.

1. What is one principle that has guided you in your life? Write about this topic for ten minutes. Don't worry about grammar or spelling. Just write down all your ideas and examples from your life. After you finish, complete the following outline.

Title: _____

Introduction: _____

    Identify yourself and where you work or study: _____

Guiding Principle: _____

    Supporting reason or example: _____

    Result: _____

Conclusion: _____

2. Organize your short speech. Use your outline. Add interesting ideas or examples. Work with a partner and practice giving your speech. Make changes as needed.

Remember to:

- clearly state your guiding principle, and give examples to show why it is important to you.
- insert signposting language for each section.
- use short pauses after signposting expressions.
- make eye contact.

Speak

Give your short speech. After you speak, answer questions from your audience.

WRITING

Read these topics. Choose one to write about.

1. Imagine that Fauci could choose only one of his guiding principles to use in his work. Which one do you think would help him the most? Why?

2. Write about the guiding principle you spoke about in the task in the Speaking section on pages 86–87.

3. Identify one specific event or accomplishment that made you feel successful. Write about how you achieved this success.

What do you believe?

As you listen to the essays in this book, think about your beliefs. Write your own *What I Believe* essay. Follow the steps on pages 132–135.

CREATIVE SOLUTIONS TO LIFE'S CHALLENGES
–Frank X Walker

GETTING READY

`CD 2 Track 16` Listen and read about the essayist.

> **Meet Frank X Walker**
>
> Frank X Walker teaches English at a university. He respects creativity. Walker believes that the challenges in his life have brought out his creative abilities. As a child, he used words creatively to save himself from neighborhood bullies.[1] For Walker, art and creativity are basic things that we can see and use in everyday life.

[1] people who hurt weaker people or make them afraid

Connect to the Topic

Discuss this situation with a partner.

In his essay, Frank X Walker says that many of life's challenges need creative solutions. Think of a creative solution to this common challenge: Your neighbor plays loud music late at night. The music keeps you and others from sleeping.

GLOSSARY

You will hear these words and expressions in the essay. Read the words and definitions before you listen.

Ethnic dolls from Zimbabwe

survival skills /səˈvaɪvəl skɪlz/ *n.* abilities used to live

creativity at work /ˌkrieɪˈtɪvət̮i ət wɚk/ *exp.* using new ideas to solve problems

ethnic /ˈɛθnɪk/ *adj.* relating to a specific cultural group

quality of life /ˈkwɑlət̮i əv laɪf/ *n.* level of comfort at which one lives, often used with *high* or *low*

rhyming couplet /ˈraɪmɪŋ ˈkʌplɪt/ *n.* two phrases or statements in which the last two words sound alike

LISTENING

Listen for Main Ideas

CD 2 Track 17 Read the question and answer choices. Then listen to Frank X Walker's essay. Circle the letter of the best answer to the question.

What is the main reason the author believes in creativity?

a. It helps us forget our problems.

b. It helps us find answers to problems in life.

c. It keeps our lives normal.

d. It makes neighborhoods safer.

Vocabulary for Comprehension

CD 2 Track 19 Read and listen to these sentences. Then circle the letter of the word or phrase closest in meaning to the boldfaced words and expressions.

1. When José left his home for college, he had to eat in the cafeteria where the food was not very good. After that, he **appreciated** his mother's cooking.

   a. understood and enjoyed

   b. didn't want to eat

2. Ken lives in a big city and is a student. All the noises from the street **distract** him while he is studying. He can only study for 15 minutes at a time.

   a. cause his attention to go in a different direction

   b. cause him to feel happy about something new or different

3. When Marta was a young girl, her father took her to his tennis games. He saw how interested she was in the sport and **encouraged** her to play tennis. Marta is now a good player.

   a. made her not want

   b. helped her become confident enough

4. When Maria's family decorates the house for Christmas, they depend on everyone's **participation**. Her parents can't do it alone.

   a. taking part in something

   b. not wanting to do something

5. When Aiyuko was young, her drawings were very **expressive**. If she used dark colors, she was upset. If she used bright colors, she was happy.

   a. unclear because she does not give enough details

   b. clear about what she thinks or feels

6. Sam's mother always says, "Children who follow the rules **deserve** some ice cream."

   a. should get

   b. should not get

7. People in some countries don't have the **right** to express their opinions. The government won't let them.

   a. something allowed by law

   b. courage

8. We can usually find Jim in his room with a pen, pad of paper, and his guitar. He is often **composing** songs or poems. He's very good with words.

   a. listening to

   b. writing

9. I have tried to write songs and poems. But they sound very **juvenile**, as if a young child had written them.

   a. immature

   b. lovely

10. Joe believes he would lose his **sanity** and become depressed if he didn't listen to music, exercise, and eat well. These things help him stay healthy.

    a. ability to work hard and quickly

    b. ability to think in a normal and sensible way

Listen for Details

A CD 2 Track 20 Read these sentences. Then listen to Walker's essay again. Check (✓) the one idea Walker <u>does not</u> mention.

1. Walker believes creativity is _____.

   ☑ working in an art gallery

   ☐ survival skills

   ☐ creative expression of living

2. Walker's mother _____.

- [ ] was a very creative cook
- [ ] encouraged children to be creative
- [ ] sang every Sunday in church

3. Walker believes that happy children are those who _____.

- [ ] take classes they like
- [ ] have freedom to express themselves
- [ ] can discover and create by themselves

4. Walker says that art and creative expression are _____.

- [ ] found only in art galleries
- [ ] everywhere and in everyone
- [ ] something people deserve

5. Comic books helped Walker to _____.

- [ ] become a bully
- [ ] find some intelligent heroes
- [ ] create his first art collection

6. Walker believes creativity can change the way we _____.

- [ ] think
- [ ] operate
- [ ] speak

7. Celebrating creativity around us helps _____.

- [ ] us find a reason for a party
- [ ] keep us happy
- [ ] maintain our sanity

In his essay, Walker mentions the following terms to talk about his experiences while growing up.

refrigerator door masterpieces children's artwork placed on the refrigerator door, usually by their parents

"Idle hands and minds are the devil's workshop" a saying often used by religious people to mean: If you are not busy, you will get into trouble

auto detailers people who carefully clean or paint the inside and outside of cars

janitors people who clean buildings or schools

sculptors people who make art from stone, wood, or clay

spiked hair a style in which hair stands up straight

cornrows a style in which hair is braided close to the head

shoelace artistry placing laces in shoes so they are different from the normal pattern, or using brightly colored or decorated laces

projects housing paid for by the government, usually in poor areas of large cities, called "the inner city"

Walker also mentions the following comic book terms in his essay.

The Black Panther (1966) and Luke Cage (1972) comic book characters

superpowers abilities given to superheroes in comic books, such as flying or having extraordinary strength

Mother and daughter with cornrows

B `CD 2 Track 21` Listen to the essay again. Complete the statements with information from the essay.

1. Give three examples of things Walker's mother did to express herself creatively.

She (a) _____,

(b) _____, and

(c) _____.

2. Every Christmas season Walker would _____.

3. According to Walker, artists include _____

_____.

4. Walker would defend himself against neighborhood bullies by _____

_____.

REACTING TO THE ESSAY

Discuss your answers to these questions.

1. Walker teaches literature at a university. Does this job require a person to be creative? What other jobs require a person to be creative? What jobs do not require creativity? Explain.

2. Walker mentions "refrigerator door masterpieces." Have you ever created something that was put up for everyone to see? What was it? If not, would you like to create something for everyone to see? Explain.

3. Walker ends by saying, "I believe creativity can help maintain our sanity and keeps us happy." Do you agree with him? Explain.

SPEAKING

In his essay, Frank X Walker states his belief in celebrating creativity in everyday life. In this section, you will describe a person whom you think is creative in an everyday way and relate it to a past experience.

Build Fluency

Language: *Would* for Repeated Actions in the Past

To talk about repeated actions in the past, use *would* and *would be* + verb + *-ing*.

REPEATED ACTIONS IN THE PAST WITH WOULD

would + base form of verb	**Examples:**
Use *would* + base form to show a past action that happened repeatedly, or with regular frequency.	When we were young, my mother **would make** dolls and dresses for my sisters.
When using more than one verb, you do not need to repeat *would*.	She **would flip** her old sewing machine upright, **study** pictures in books and magazines, and then **make** ethnic versions of those same dolls and stuffed animals to sell at church fund-raisers.
Use *would be* + verb + *-ing* to indicate that a repeated action happened while another event was taking place.	My mother **would be making** hot chocolate for us in the kitchen while we **would play** outside in the snow.

PRACTICE Complete the story. Put the verbs in parentheses in the correct form. Use *would* or *would be* + verb + *-ing*.

My best friend Ellen is a creative person. We were roommates for four years in college. When we were at home, she (1) *would do* (do) many things. For example, she (2) _____ (put together) photo albums or (3) _____ (design) birthday cards. While she was doing those things, I (4) _____ (cook). Every weekend, we (5) _____ (invite) some friends over. Ellen (6) _____ (play) the guitar for us. She (7) _____ (make up) songs as she played. Everyone (8) _____ (sing) and (9) _____ (laugh) for hours. We had a lot of fun. Ellen was always very creative, and she liked to share her talents with her friends.

Pronunciation: Contracted *Would*

> **CD 2 Track 22** Use the contracted form of *would* in conversational English. The contracted form is *'d*. It is pronounced /d/ at the end of the subject. It is possible to contract *would* after names, but it is most common to contract *would* after subject pronouns. Listen to the example.
>
> EXAMPLE:
>
> On Saturdays in the summer, he**'d** be cooking dinner while I**'d** paint.

A PRACTICE Listen to these examples. Write the contracted pronoun you hear.

1. _____*I'd*_____ go grocery shopping every Saturday morning.

2. _____ always sing in the evenings.

3. _____ always drive me to school in the morning.

4. _____ be studying at the library while _____ be cleaning the apartment.

5. _____ walk home together after school.

6. _____ be talking during lectures.

B PRACTICE Work with a partner. Go back to the Practice exercise on page 96 and read the story aloud. Use contractions where possible.

Get Ready to Speak

TASK

Describing a Person

Talk about a creative person whom you know or knew in the past. Explain how this person showed his or her creativity in everyday life.

1. Choose a creative person in your life to speak about. Make a list of all the things that make her or him creative. Think about the times when this person did something in particular that showed how creative he or she is.

2. Organize your ideas. Work with a partner. Tell your partner about this creative person. Make changes as needed.

Remember to:

- talk about why you think the person was or is creative. Talk about the times when the person did something that showed his or her creativity.
- use *would* to talk about repeated actions in the past.
- use *would be* + verb + *-ing* to talk about repeated past actions that happened at the same time as another activity.
- use contractions of *would* where appropriate.

Speak

Present your talk about the creative person to the class or in a small group. After speaking, answer questions from your audience.

WRITING

Read these topics. Choose one to write about.

1. Imagine you are writing a letter to a friend about Frank X Walker. Describe why you think he is creative. Write about creative activities he did when he was a boy as well as what he does now.

2. Write about the person you chose to speak about in the Speaking section on pages 97–98. Describe why you think he or she is creative. In your description, include creative things the person did in the past.

3. Write about a challenging time in your life that required a creative solution. What was the challenge? How did you resolve it? Why was the solution creative?

What do you believe?

As you listen to the essays in this book, think about your beliefs. Write your own *What I Believe* essay. Follow the steps on pages 132–135.

FREE MINDS AND HEARTS AT WORK
–Jackie Robinson

GETTING READY

CD 2 Track 23 Listen and read about the essayist.

Meet Jackie Robinson

In 1947, Jackie Robinson became the first African-American to play in Major League Baseball. Baseball was the most popular sport in the United States at this time. Robinson experienced a lot of unfair treatment because he was black. Many people told him he should not play baseball. Robinson was able to overcome these challenges because of his beliefs.

Connect to the Topic

Discuss these questions with a partner.

Jackie Robinson experienced unfair treatment because of his race when he joined Major League Baseball. In what situations have you seen people treated unfairly? What happened? How did it make you feel?

GLOSSARY

You will hear these words and expressions in the essay. Read their definitions before you listen.

imperfections /ˌɪmpɚˈfɛkʃənz/ n. mistakes in things, including behavior

handicaps /ˈhændiˌkæps/ n. conditions or situations that make it difficult for someone to do something

stumbling blocks /ˈstʌmbəlɪŋ blɑks/ n. problems preventing a person from achieving something; also **obstacles** n.

prejudices /ˈprɛdʒədɪsɪs/ n. unfair feelings of dislike against someone who is of a different race, sex, or religion

obstacles /ˈɑbstɪkəlz/ n. things that make success difficult

dogmas /ˈdɔgməz/ n. beliefs people are expected to accept as true, without questioning them

barriers /ˈbæriɚz/ n. social attitudes or beliefs that keep some people from doing things

LISTENING

Listen for Main Ideas

CD 2 Track 24 Read these sentences. Then listen to Jackie Robinson's essay. Check (✓) the main ideas.

☐ 1. Jackie Robinson fought social obstacles to play baseball.

☐ 2. Major League Baseball invited all minorities to play in Atlanta.

☐ 3. People are not perfect.

☐ 4. Robinson always believed there was a chance he would win his fight.

☐ 5. Robinson doesn't believe his children will have to fight against social obstacles.

☐ 6. Robinson never gave up hope because of his belief in a free society.

Vocabulary for Comprehension

CD 2 Track 26 Read and listen to these sentences. Circle the letter of the word or phrase closest in meaning to the boldfaced words and expressions.

1. **In the scheme of** human events, it was time for African-Americans to be treated more fairly.

   a. in the general view of (a situation)
   b. in the beginning of (a situation)

2. In a country where freedom and justice are very important, prejudice and racism have to **be reckoned with**.

   a. be recognized as something valuable
   b. be faced with or confronted as a problem

3. Some black people worked a very long time for fair treatment. It was hard work. They were **sustained** by the belief that things would eventually change for the better.

   a. supported
   b. stopped

4. When racism and prejudice are **deep-rooted**, it takes generations for change to happen.

   a. fair and open-minded
   b. strong and difficult to change

5. In a **free society**, a person can feel safe even if his or her ideas are not popular or common.

   a. society where people can express their views without fear of arrest, imprisonment, or physical harm
   b. society where people have a right to vote, but only for one person

6. If we keep working hard, there is a high **probability** that one day soon we will receive fair treatment.

   a. uncertain time
   b. possibility

7. Over the past 60 years, people in the United States have fought for their civil rights. Many have **attained** these rights. Some have not.

   a. bought
   b. achieved

8. Laws in this country are not **static**. They are continually changing, so we have to keep ourselves educated.

   a. the same, unchanging
   b. continually unbalanced

9. Not everyone joined the fight for equal rights, but most people with **integrity** did.

   a. wealth or a lot of land
   b. honesty and high morals

10. If you believe that what you are fighting for is **doomed**, you will probably not succeed.

    a. certain to fail

    b. likely to change

Listen for Details

A CD 2 Track 27 Read these sentences. Then listen to Robinson's essay again. Circle the word or phrase that best completes each sentence.

1. At the beginning of the World Series in 1947, Robinson was happy because he was (included / excluded).

2. A year later, blacks and whites played baseball together (for the first time / one last time).

3. According to Robinson, (perfection / imperfection) is a human quality.

4. In Robinson's opinion, handicaps, stumbling blocks, and prejudices (are / are not) part of life.

5. Robinson believed in his fight to join Major League Baseball because he knew society was (prejudiced / changing).

6. The obstacles and prejudices Robinson faced (defeated him / made him fight more).

7. Robinson says he believes his children have a chance for a better future because many of the (dogmas / guarantees) will have vanished by the time they are adults.

8. In order for a society to remain good, Robinson believes people must be (doomed / willing) to fight for it.

B CD 2 Track 28 Read these statements. Listen to the essay again. Circle the letter of the sentence that is closest in meaning to Robinson's quotes.

1. "And I thought: What I have always believed has come to be."

    a. My belief has come true.

    b. My belief hasn't come true.

2. "... wherever human beings were given room to breathe and time to think, those imperfections would disappear, no matter how slowly."

   a. In a society where people are able to move and think freely, mistakes would eventually be corrected.

   b. It takes too long for mistakes to go away because people just talk about them, rather than doing something about them.

3. "... they will never face some of these prejudices because other people have gone before them."

   a. They won't have to fight against these prejudices because there won't be any prejudice when they are adults.

   b. They won't have to fight some of these prejudices because things have started to change already.

REACTING TO THE ESSAY

Discuss your answers to these questions.

1. Robinson says that where humans are "given room to breathe and time to think," imperfections disappear. What do you think he means by this? Explain in your own words. Do you agree? Explain.

2. Robinson talks about preparing his kids to meet obstacles and prejudices in life. How do you think he did that?

3. Robinson experienced unfair treatment when he joined Major League Baseball. Imagine being at a sports game and seeing someone sent away because of their race. How would you feel about this? What would you do?

CULTURE NOTES

Jackie Robinson lived through a time of great change in the United States known as the Civil Rights Movement. Many believe that his "breaking the color barrier" in Major League Baseball in 1947 helped to start this movement, which began a few years later.

Read the time line that highlights some events in Jackie Robinson's life.

Jackie Robinson

1919	born in Cairo, Georgia
1942–45	served in the U.S. Army
1947	was the first black man to play in Major League Baseball
1956	retired from Major League Baseball
1962	inducted into the Baseball Hall of Fame
1972	died on October 24
1973	Jackie Robinson Foundation established to help minority students go to college

SPEAKING

In his essay, Jackie Robinson states his belief that human imperfections can be overcome when people are given room and time to think. In this section, you will plan and present your predictions about two imperfections or social problems that society will overcome in the next 100 years.

Build Fluency

Language: Future and Future Perfect

Use the future tense to make general predictions. Use the future perfect tense to make predictions about events that will happen by a specific time in the future.

MAKING PREDICTIONS	
Future *Will* + base form of the verb Use the future verb tense to make predictions about the future.	**Example:** In the future, men and women **will receive** equal pay for equal work.
Future Perfect *Will* + have + past participle Use the future perfect to talk about an event that will be completed before a specific time or event in the future.	**Examples:** By the year 2100, we **will have resolved** racism in the workplace. In 100 years, we **will have created** a health care system for all people.

PRACTICE Read each sentence. Then circle the letter of the sentence that is similar in meaning.

1. By the year 2014, we will have completed our studies.

    a. We will be done studying before the year 2014.
    b. We will finish studying after the year 2014.

2. By the time my children are adults, they will have moved away from home.

    a. They will be living in a different place.
    b. They will be living at home.

3. By the year 2020, my granddaughter will have graduated from university.

    a. She will graduate in the year 2020 or before.
    b. She will graduate after 2020.

4. We will have improved our study skills by January.

    a. We will still be improving our study skills in January.
    b. We will be finished improving our study skills by January.

5. In fifty years, I will have stopped working.

    a. Fifty years from now, I will not be working.

    b. Fifty years from now, I will still be working.

6. It's the year 2010. In 2014, you will have finished studying in your English courses.

    a. In 2014, you will have to study English for two more years.

    b. You will not have to take any more English courses after 2014.

Pronunciation: Contractions with *Will*

> **CD 2 Track 29** To contract the future perfect, join the subject pronoun and *will* together. The contracted *[l]* changes the vowel of the subject pronouns *I, you, he, she, we,* and *they* from long to short. With the subject pronoun *it*, there is no vowel change. An extra vowel, schwa /ə/, gets inserted before the *[l]*. Listen to the examples.
>
> EXAMPLES:
>
> I + will → I'll   we + will → we'll
>
> you + will → you'll   they + will → they'll
>
> he + will → he'll
>
> she + will → she'll
>
> it + will → it'll

A PRACTICE Read the description predicting how long it will take a group of people to read a magazine article. Then read it aloud with a partner.

    It's 10:00 in the morning right now. I'm reading an article about Jackie Robinson. *I'll* have finished the article in ten minutes. Then you can read it. In twenty minutes, *you'll* have read it and *you'll* give it to Martin. *He'll* have read it in thirty minutes, and then Rebecca will read it. *She'll* have read it in forty minutes. *It'll* be 10:40 by the time *we'll* all have read it. Then we can talk about it to our friends, and *they'll* want to read it, too.

B PRACTICE Rewrite the sentences in the Practice exercise on pages 106–107. Contract all the pronouns and *will* in the correct answers. Alternate reading them aloud with a partner.

Get Ready to Speak

TASK

Predicting

Predict two social problems that society will have overcome in 100 years. Describe the problems and explain why you think they will be overcome.

1. Answer the questions about two social problems in the chart.

Questions	Problem 1	Problem 2
What is the problem? How big a problem is it? Has it already improved somewhat in past years? Who is affected by the problem? How would things be better if the problem disappeared? What do you think needs to be done to help the problem go away?		

2. Work with a partner. Practice giving your predictions. Include all of the information you wrote in your chart. Make changes as needed.

Remember to:

- use the future or future perfect verb tenses.

- use contractions with subject pronouns and *will*.

Speak

Present your predictions about social problems to the class or in small groups.

WRITING

Read these topics. Choose one to write about.

1. Write about one or all of the social problems that you spoke about in the Speaking section on pages 108–109.

2. Go back and read question 2 in the Reacting to the Essay section on page 104. Write the conversation between Robinson and his children. What do you think he would say to his children to help prepare them to overcome future obstacles and prejudices?

3. Robinson says he found imperfection in baseball and fought it. Have you found imperfection in another area of life and fought it? Where was that imperfection and how did you fight it?

What do you believe?

As you listen to the essays in this book, think about your beliefs. Write your own *What I Believe* essay. Follow the steps on pages 132–135.

IN GIVING I CONNECT WITH OTHERS
–Isabel Allende

GETTING READY

CD 2 Track 30 Listen and read about the essayist.

Meet Isabel Allende

Isabel Allende was born in Peru and raised in Chile. She is best known for writing novels. Her personal philosophy of life has been shaped by her experiences with her family. One experience in particular made her write a book and this essay. Her daughter, Paula, died in 1992. After losing Paula, Allende realized an important belief. She applies this belief to her daily life.

Connect to the Topic

Discuss these questions with a partner.

- Isabel Allende's daughter, Paula, was a volunteer. She worked to help poor women and children.

- Do you (or does someone you know) volunteer to help others in the community? Where?

- If someone told you he or she wanted to volunteer, what kind of advice would you give that person?

GLOSSARY

You will hear these words and expressions in the essay. Read their definitions before you listen.

coma /ˈkoʊmə/ *n.* the condition of not being awake for a long time, usually after an accident or illness

agony /ˈægəni/ *n.* extreme pain or suffering

grieving /ˈgrivɪŋ/ *n.* feeling very sad for a period of time, usually after the death of a loved one

paralyzed /ˈpærəˌlaɪzd/ *adj.* not being able to move the body

let go (of) /lɛt goʊ əv/ *v.* stop holding someone or something

cling (to) /klɪŋ tu/ *v.* be dependent on someone or their beliefs

LISTENING

Listen for Main Ideas

CD 2 Track 31 Read this question and these sentences. Then listen to Isabel Allende's essay. Circle the letter of the answer to this question.

Which statement best summarizes Allende's belief?

a. It's better to receive than to give.

b. Share your experiences, but within limits.

c. Giving is life's greatest joy and keeps our loved ones in our hearts.

d. People should volunteer to help their communities.

Vocabulary for Comprehension

CD 2 Track 33 Read and listen to the letter from the Women's and Children's Organization of Northern California. Discuss the meanings of the boldfaced words. Then match the words with their definitions on page 113.

Women's and Children's Organization of Northern California

333 Northern Sunset Lane

San Francisco, CA

I am the assistant director of the Women's and Children's Organization of Northern California (WCONC). Last year, we received a $20,000 grant from the Isabel Allende Foundation. I would like to (a) **reflect on** how this grant has helped us.

First, our (b) **principles** have always included helping women and children when they most need it. Our director decided to reduce her salary to avoid shutting down a breakfast program for kids in school. With the grant money, we don't have to worry about eliminating our community programs any longer. The grant helps us keep (c) **consistency** in our programs: The WCONC can be there to help women and children when they need us most.

Second, the Isabel Allende Foundation has inspired our new (d) **mantra**: "There's no time like the present to give."

Finally, this grant allows us to reach out to women in difficult situations. These women often think they must remain (e) **independent**; often they don't trust others. We must reach out to them. We work with them to rebuild the lives they (f) **crave**: working and providing for their children while they participate in their communities in meaningful ways.

This has all been made possible by the hard work of our staff, and the Isabel Allende Foundation.

1. _____ relying only on themselves

2. _____ guiding ideas

3. _____ quality of always staying the same

4. _____ want very much

5. _____ repeated word or group of words

6. _____ think carefully and for a long time about something

Listen for Details

A **CD 2 Track 34** Read these sentences. Then listen to Allende's essay again. Check (✓) *True, False,* or *Don't Know.*

Sentence	True	False	Don't Know
1. Allende thought about her beliefs during her daughter's illness.	✓	☐	☐
2. Before Paula's illness, Allende didn't think about her beliefs much.	☐	☐	☐
3. According to Allende, you have to give so you can feel a variety of feelings.	☐	☐	☐
4. As a volunteer, Allende's daughter, Paula, needed lots of things.	☐	☐	☐
5. Since her daughter's death, Allende no longer clings to anything.	☐	☐	☐
6. Allende prefers to give rather than to receive.	☐	☐	☐
7. Allende's family and dog don't like her.	☐	☐	☐
8. According to Allende, spending money is a way of showing love.	☐	☐	☐

B CD 2 Track 35 Read these sentences. Listen to the essay again. Does Allende mention these examples of giving? Circle *Yes* or *No*.

1. taking care of her daughter at home		Yes	No
2. advising women with children on legal issues		Yes	No
3. spending time teaching computer skills to the elderly		Yes	No
4. sharing experience, knowledge, talent, and wealth		Yes	No

REACTING TO THE ESSAY

Discuss your answers to these questions.

1. When talking about her family, Allende says, "I adore my husband, my son, my grandchildren, my mother, my dog, and frankly I don't know if they even like me. But who cares? Loving them is my joy." What do you think about Allende's attitude? Is this a good attitude to have toward those you love? Explain.

2. Allende gives by telling stories. What other ways can people give in the way that Allende talks about?

3. In which professions is it important to be a giver? For example, can a person be a good nurse if she or he is not giving? Explain.

BACKGROUND NOTES

Read the timeline highlighting some events in Isabel Allende's life.

1942   She is born in Lima, Peru, where her father, Tomás, was Chilean ambassador

1963   Her daughter Paula is born.

1967   She begins her writing career.

1982   Her first novel *House of the Spirits* is published in Spain.

1992   Paula passes away.

1994   *Paula*, a memoir of Isabel's early life, is published in Spain.

1996   The Isabel Allende Foundation is formed in memory of her daughter.

Isabel Allende and her husband Willie Gordon

Today, Isabel Allende and her husband live in San Francisco, CA, near her son, Nicolás, and his family.

SPEAKING

Isabel Allende's mantra is "You only have what you give." The life her daughter chose as a volunteer inspired Allende to give more of herself. In this section, you will interview each other about your own or others' volunteer experience.

Build Fluency

Language: Infinitives

Some verbs and verb phrases are followed by the infinitive (*to* + base form of verb).

EXPLAINING ACTIONS: INFINITIVES	
Verb + infinitive:	EXAMPLES:
hope	As a volunteer, Laura **hopes** *to help* many poor families.
want	She **wants** *to volunteer* six days a week.
decide	Laura **decided** *to help* them because she knew no one else would.
find time	She always **finds time** *to spend* with poor families.
have an opportunity	People are happy they **have an opportunity** *to work* with Laura.
Verb + object + infinitive:	EXAMPLES:
inspire	Laura's parents **inspired** her *to volunteer*.
encourage	They **encouraged** her *to donate* her time and talent.
expect	She **expected** them *to help* when possible.

PRACTICE Put the verbs in parentheses into the correct form. Some may require objects.

1. Ken finds time _to cook_ (cook) at the local community center once a month.

2. The other volunteers think he's a great cook. He inspired _____ (learn) how to cook.

3. Ken decided _____ (offer) a cooking class to staff and visitors.

4. He hopes _____ (teach) it once a week for a month.

5. Sara wanted _____ (attend) the class but had to take care of her sick daughter.

6. She says she will try _____ (come) next month.

7. Sara's husband encouraged _____ (call) Ken and ask about next month's class.

8. Ken knows Sara is also a good cook. He expects _____ (give) advice) on cooking techniques, too, because she knows a lot about food.

9. Many people came to Ken and Sara's cooking class. Sara helped_____ (cook) tomato sauce for pasta.

10. Everyone was glad he or she had an opportunity _____ (learn) together.

Pronunciation: Reduction of *To*

> **CD 2 Track 36** In conversation, the *to* of infinitives is often reduced. We do not always hear the /u/ (as in *to*). Instead, the *o* in *to* is sometimes reduced to schwa /ə/. Listen to the examples.
>
> EXAMPLES:
> 1. I've decided to donate my time at the food bank.
> 2. To find volunteer opportunities, just ask your friends.

A PRACTICE Listen to these sentences. Circle the words that are reduced.

1. Paula was a great volunteer. She dedicated her time to help poor people.

2. John called the center to get more information.

3. They encouraged him to help two times a week.

4. To help those who need it most, the center welcomes women and children.

5. He said he would try to find time.

B PRACTICE Work with a partner. Go back to the Practice exercise on page 116 and read the sentences aloud. Reduce the infinitives.

Get Ready to Speak

TASK

Talking about Experiences

Do you or someone you know volunteer? Respond to questions about volunteer experiences. Tell others about those experiences.

1. Take three minutes. Make notes about your or another person's volunteer experience. What kind of work is it? Why did you or someone you know decide to volunteer?

2. Interview a partner about volunteering.

1. What kind of volunteer work is it?

2. Why did you or someone you know decide to volunteer?

3. How do you or someone you know find the time to volunteer?

4. Did anyone inspire you or someone you know to volunteer?

5. What would you say to encourage others to volunteer?

Use these expressions, or interjections to respond to comments. Then move on to the next topic.

USEFUL EXPRESSIONS

Responding to Comments

Really? How interesting. Now . . .

That's amazing. So . . .

Wow! What a story. My next question . . .

3. Organize your ideas. Insert verbs and infinitives where necessary. Practice giving your talk to another pair of students. Each partner should speak for about the same amount of time. Make changes as needed.

Remember to:

• use verbs and infinitives.

• reduce the pronunciation of the *to* of infinitives.

• use the useful expressions when responding to people's comments.

Speak

Talk about the volunteer experience to the class or your group. Compare experiences.

WRITING

Read the topics. Choose one to write about.

1. Isabel Allende says she gives away her stories. Do you think she might help people through her writing? How? Give one example.

2. Write about the topic you spoke about in the Speaking section on pages 117–119.

3. Why do people volunteer? List all the of possible reasons. Give an example for each reason.

4. Think of a volunteer project for your class. Identify the project, the number of hours, and resources. Explain why you think the class should participate.

What do you believe?

As you listen to the essays in this book, think about your beliefs. Write your own *What I Believe* essay. Follow the steps on pages 132–135.

A BALANCE BETWEEN NATURE AND NURTURE
–Gloria Steinem

GETTING READY

CD 2 Track 37 Listen and read about the essayist.

Meet Gloria Steinem

Gloria Steinem is a journalist. She became well-known in the United States in the1960s and 1970s for speaking out in favor of equality for women. In her essay, Steinem discusses the nature-nurture debate. This debate has two points of view. Those who believe in "nature" believe that children are born a certain way (with certain qualities). Supporters of "nurture" believe outside factors influence children's behavior. Steinem presents her answer to the nature-nurture question.

Connect to the Topic

Discuss these questions with a partner.

Think about some of the characteristics of some the essayists in this book. Where did these characteristics come from? Why did they do the things they did? What influenced them more: nature or nurture? Place a check (✓) in the column that matches your opinion. Explain your choices.

Unit and Essayist	Trait	Nature	Nurture
Unit 1 Harold Taw	Taw follows a tradition year after year. Taw is a traditional person.		
Unit 5 Gregory Orr	Orr writes poetry to cope with life's challenges. He uses language creatively to shape his life's experiences.		
Unit 9 Frank X Walker	Walker is creative with language. He believes that creativity is a powerful way to deal with life's challenges.		
Unit 10 Jackie Robinson	Robinson believes that we can overcome human imperfections. He is optimistic.		
Unit 11 Isabel Allende	Allende gives what she has to others. She is generous.		
Other:			

GLOSSARY

You will hear these words and expressions in the essay. Read their definitions before you listen.

gender /'dʒɛndɚ/ n. state of being either male or
    female

adolescent /ˌædl'ɛsənt/ n. used to describe a period
    of life between 13–17 years of age

conform /kən 'fɔrm/ v. behave in a way that most
    people act

**A group of adolescent
high school students**

stage /steɪdʒ/ n. period of time as someone grows and develops

hierarchies /'haɪə, rɑrkiz/ n. systems of power in society and government

blank slates /blæŋk sleɪts/ n. idea that children are empty and need to be
    filled with information

LISTENING

Listen for Main Ideas

CD 2 Track 38 Read these sentences. Then listen to Gloria Steinem's essay. Check (✓) the three sentences that express Steinem's main ideas.

- ☐ a. Each generation must learn the same lessons.

- ☐ b. Some people think children are influenced only by heredity.

- ☐ c. Women should challenge ideas about their place in society.

- ☐ d. Some people think kids are selfish and therefore need lots of rules.

- ☐ e. Children don't understand what is fair and what is not fair.

- ☐ f. Steinem believes children are a balance of nature and nurture.

Vocabulary for Comprehension

CD 2 Track 40 Read these words and phrases and their definitions. Use the words and phrases to complete the sentences below. Then listen to the sentences and check your answers.

---

former *adj.* the first thing mentioned; (*opp.* **latter** *adj.* the last thing mentioned)

enlightening *adj.* instructive; intellectually informing someone

textbook space *exp.* information on pages or chapters in school books

obsessions *n.* persistent, dominant ideas that do not go away

race and class complexities *exp.* relations that are difficult to understand between people from different cultures or social statuses

civilizing *adj.* having the effect of making someone behave more politely

controls *n.* rules to make someone behave in a certain way

---

1. The lecture Steve attended on feminism was very _____. He never knew that feminism was responsible for equal pay between men and women.

2. Nora's high school has a very diverse student population. There are people from all over the world and different economic backgrounds. Needless to say, there are many _____.

3. Carla and Janet are twins with different personalities. Carla is shy, but Janet is talkative. The _____ doesn't speak very often, and the _____ is always chatting with someone.

4. Steinem doesn't believe children need a lot of _____ in order to become well-behaved adults. In fact, she thinks they can actually make them destructive.

5. History books in American classrooms today give more _____ to world history than they did fifty years ago.

6. John's school made a lot of rules to follow at sports events. They thought the rules would have a _____ effect on the students, but in fact, more students got into trouble than before.

7. Teenagers in high school have a lot of _____: They often worry about what kind of music to listen to and the type of clothes they should wear. They think a lot about being accepted by their friends.

Listen for Details

A **CD 2 Track 41** Read these sentences. Then listen to Steinem's essay again. Circle the letter of the answer that best completes each sentence.

1. She grew up mostly _____.
   a. around books
   b. around grown-ups

2. Her first experience in public school made her feel _____.
   a. unprepared
   b. afraid

3. As an adolescent, Steinem tried to _____.
   a. conform to popular ideas
   b. act in theatrical productions

4. She began to find her own voice again when _____.
   a. she remembered President Kennedy
   b. she went to India for two years

5. The feminist movement questioned the idea that _____.
   a. what happened to men could be changed, but what happened to women could not
   b. what happened to men was not fair, but what happened to women was fair

6. According to Steinem, young kids naturally seem to expect _____.

   a. fairness

   b. people to help them

7. According to Steinem, the conservative message about children is that

   _____.

   a. they need to be controlled

   b. they need to understand themselves

8. Steinem thinks the liberal message about children is that _____.

   a. children start with empty minds and society will fill them

   b. children should be able to run free and make their own rules

9. Steinem believes that we might start to see great possibilities for society if

   _____.

   a. we had a balanced view on the nature vs. nurture issue

   b. we raised one generation with respect and no violence

B **CD 2 Track 42** Listen to the essay again. Complete these sentences.

1. Steinem was unprepared for school at age twelve because _____

   _____

   _____

2. When she and other women began to gather, they _____

   _____

   _____

3. Steinem doesn't believe in either the conservative or the liberal message about
children. On the contrary, she believes _____

   _____

   _____

REACTING TO THE ESSAY

Discuss your answers to these questions.

1. Steinem talks about "adolescents trying to conform." Do most teenagers want to be like other teenagers? Explain.

2. Steinem concludes her essay with two questions: "What would happen if we listened to children as much as we talked to them? What would happen if even one generation were raised with respect and without violence?" What do you think would happen?

3. Now that you have listened to and analyzed the essay, would you change any of your answers to the question in the Connect to the Topic section on page 121? Explain.

BACKGROUND NOTES

Steinem discusses these topics in her essay.

The Feminist Movement: During the 1960s and 1970s in the United States, feminists successfully protested and demanded equal economic, political, and social opportunities for women.

Gandhians: The followers of Mohandas Gandhi (1869–1948) in India. Gandhi led large, nonviolent protests to gain independence from British India. India became an independent nation in 1947.

The Kennedys: A famous, wealthy, and politically active Irish-American family. The most well-known Kennedy is John F. Kennedy, who was president of the United States from 1961–63.

Women's rights march with Gloria Steinem—October 7, 1995 in New York City

SPEAKING

Steinem believes that children develop best with a balanced understanding of nature and nurture. Their education and development must consider nature (characteristics they are born with), and nurture (their environment). In this section, you will plan and conduct a debate about the issue of nature vs. nurture.

Build Fluency

Language: Expressing Strong Arguments

Debating means making a strong argument for your point of view. First, make a point. Then, use one of the expressions below to make your point stronger.

Furthermore, moreover, in addition, needless to say, therefore, so, and *as a result* are **transitions**. They come after a statement. They are used at the beginning of a clause and followed by a comma (,) in writing.

EXPRESSING STRONG ARGUMENTS	
Use *furthermore*, *moreover*, and *in addition* to add more details to your argument.	EXAMPLE: **Furthermore,** **Moreover,** } they already have so **In addition,** } many rules to follow.
Use *needless to say* to make an obvious, but strong point.	EXAMPLE: **Needless to say**, uniforms are boring.
Use *so, therefore,* and *as a result* to show a result or conclusion.	EXAMPLE: **Therefore**, children should be allowed to wear what they want.

Steinem's Ideas	For "Nature"	For "Nurture"
1. ". . . children are naturally selfish and destructive creatures who need civilizing by hierarchies or painful controls."		
2. ". . . hierarchy and painful controls create destructive people."		
3. ". . . children are blank slates on which society can write anything."		

2. Use Steinem's ideas from the chart, along with your own ideas, to debate the issue of nature or nurture. Review the examples in your chart. Insert transitions for making strong arguments. Divide into teams. Plan who will say what for your team.

3. Practice explaining your side of the issue with another group. Make changes, as needed.

Remember to:

- use transitions for strengthening arguments.
- use the correct word stress on transitions.

Speak

Get into your debate teams. Present your side of the debate and defend your opinions with strong arguments. Keep in mind that you have a limited time to speak. When the debate is finished, have a class discussion to find a balance between the two opposing view points.

WRITING

Read these topics. Choose one to write about.

1. Write about one side of the nature or nurture issue that you debated in the Speaking section on pages 129–130. Explain your point of view and support it with examples.

2. Refer to question 2 in the Reacting to the Essay section on page 126. Write about ways adolescents try to conform. Explain how conforming does or does not help their development into adults.

3. Write a detailed answer to Steinem's question: "What would happen if we listened to children as much as we talked to them?" Use transitions.

What do you believe?

As you listen to the essays in this book, think about your beliefs. Write your own *What I Believe* essay. Follow the steps on pages 132–135.

YOUR *WHAT I BELIEVE* ESSAY

Follow these steps to write your own *What I Believe* essay.

☐ 1. **Brainstorm**

Make a list of beliefs: ideas, feelings, actions, or relationships that are important to you. Don't worry about grammar, spelling, or sentences.

☐ 2. **Refine**

Look at your list. Cross out ideas that you are not interested in writing about.

☐ 3. **Narrow the Topic**

Choose one belief on your list. Write one or two sentences that state your belief. Share it with a partner (or your teacher). Edit your sentences, as needed.

☐ 4. **Tell a Story**

Think of one or two true stories that help explain your belief. Be sure that the stories are directly connected to your belief.

☐ 5. **Add Examples and Details**

Add specific examples and details that make your story clearer or more interesting. Remember to focus on your belief.

☐ 6. **Organize**

Organize your ideas. Write a simple outline of your essay. Be sure your essay has a beginning, a middle, and an end.

☐ 7. **Write Your First Draft**

Write the first draft of your essay. Follow your outline in Step 6. Remember to:

☐ Write about what you believe, not what you don't believe.

☐ Write about yourself. Use the first person ("I").

☐ Use words and phrases that you are comfortable writing and saying.

☐ 8. **Get Feedback**

Work with a partner. Read your partner's essay. Discuss these questions.

☐ Is the belief clear and specific? Tell your partner what his/her belief is.

☐ Is the introduction interesting? Tell your partner what is interesting about it.

☐ Is the story directly connected to the belief? Tell your partner which parts do and do not help explain the belief.

☐ Is there an interesting conclusion? Is the belief restated in the conclusion? Tell your partner what you thought about after reading the last paragraph.

☐ 9. **Write Your Second Draft**

Use your partner's feedback to make changes in your essay. Write the second draft of your essay.

☐ 10. **Get Feedback**

☐ Read your essay out loud several times. Make changes, as needed.

☐ Ask a partner to listen to you read your essay. Ask for feedback. Make changes, as needed.

☐ Make a clean copy of your essay, and give your essay to your teacher for feedback.

☐ 11. **Prepare the Final Draft: Your Script**

☐ Look at your teacher's feedback. Make changes, as needed. Write the final draft of your essay.

☐ Practice reading your essay out loud.

☐ 12. **Present Your Essay**

Read your essay to your audience.

VOCABULARY

VOCABULARY UNIT-BY-UNIT

UNIT 1

burden
coast is clear, the
collective bargaining agreement
contraband
do (something) without fail
flourish
karmic
make an exception
narcissism
nourishment
overcome
ploy
poverty
prosperity
superstitious
suspected
violating

UNIT 2

bugging
common ground
crusade
embrace
envy
have a hunch
hired
inadequate
inquire
inquisitive
know where (one) stands
license
merit
muddled
no man's land
opposing arguments
quirky
shot
torn
yearning for

UNIT 3

baby grand
despair
detour
enslaved
jazz standard
lift (someone) up
moral high ground
notes
sax
sit in
terrified
tested (one's) faith
universe
vibrations
wager
welder

UNIT 4

battle
calling hours
condolence line
funeral
gesture of kindness, a
got out of
humdrum
matter of course, a
meant the world to
Shiva call
shell-shocked
stammered out
stick to
sympathy
unequivocal
versus

UNIT 5

agonizing
chaotic

cut (someone) off from
emotional chaos
grief
live by
miracle
process (n.)
process (v.)
proof
rifle
shame
transforming
traumatic
triumph

UNIT 6

accomplish
activist
back up
campaign
challenge
confront
courage
defending
glorify
irrelevant
power
responsibility
right
seek solutions
taking action
voice (one's) opinion

Unit 7

attorneys
avoid
beg (someone)
biologists
cajoling
CIA agents

embryologists
fire walkers
forensic anthropologists
have a taste for
hypnotists
keeps (someone) in the game
neurosurgeons
paraphrase
physicists
pop culture
ridiculed
subject (someone) to
tattoo
trial lawyers

UNIT 8

alleviate
anxiety
drives (someone)
focused on
inadequacy
infectious diseases
make an impact on
nagging
perfectionist
physician
potential
public health catastrophe
public service
striving
sweat the small stuff
thirst

UNIT 9

appreciated
composing
creativity at work
deserve
distract
encouraged
ethnic
expressive
juvenile
participation
quality of life
rhyming couplet
right
sanity
survival skills

UNIT 10

attained
barriers
be reckoned with
deep-rooted
dogmas
doomed
free society
handicaps
imperfections
integrity
in the scheme of
obstacles
prejudices
probability

static
stumbling blocks
sustained

UNIT 11

agony
cling to
coma
consistency
crave
grieving
independent
let go (of something)
mantra
paralyzed
principles
reflect on

UNIT 12

adolescent
blank slates
civilizing
conform
controls
enlightening
former
gender
hierarchies
obsessions
race and class complexities
stage
textbook space

VOCABULARY MASTER LIST

Numbers refer to the units in which the items occur.

accomplish, 6
activist, 6
adolescent, 12
agonizing, 5
agony, 11
alleviate, 8
anxiety, 8
appreciated, 9
attained, 10
attorneys, 7
avoid, 7
baby grand, 3
back up, 6
barriers, 10
battle, 4
be reckoned with, 10
beg (someone), 7
biologists, 7
blank slates, 12
bugging, 2
burden, 1
cajoling, 7
calling hours, 4
campaign, 6
challenge, 6
chaotic, 5
CIA agents, 7
civilizing, 12
cling to, 11
coast is clear, the, 1
collective bargaining agreement, 1
coma, 11
common ground, 2
composing, 9
condolence line, 4
conform, 12
confront, 6
consistency, 11
contraband, 1
controls, 12
courage, 6
crave, 11
creativity at work, 9
crusade, 2
cut (someone) off from, 5
deep-rooted, 10
defending, 6
deserve, 9
despair, 3
detour, 3
distract, 9
do (something) without fail, 1
dogmas, 10

doomed, 10
drives (someone), 8
embrace, 2
embryologists, 7
emotional chaos, 5
encouraged, 9
enlightening, 12
enslaved, 3
envy, 2
ethnic, 9
expressive, 9
fire walkers, 7
flourish, 1
focused on, 8
forensic anthropologists, 7
former, 12
free society, 10
funeral, 4
gender, 12
gesture of kindness, 4
glorify, 6
got out of, 4
grief, 5
grieving, 11
handicaps, 10
have a hunch, 2
have a taste for, 7
hierarchies, 12
hired, 2
humdrum, 4
hypnotists, 7
imperfections, 10
in the scheme of, 10
inadequacy, 8
inadequate, 2
independent, 11
infectious diseases, 8
inquire, 2
inquisitive, 2
integrity, 10
irrelevant, 6
jazz standard, 3
juvenile, 9
karmic, 1
keeps (someone) in the game, 7
know where (one) stands, 2
let go (of), 11
license, 2
lift (someone) up, 3
live by, 5
make an exception, 1
make an impact on, 8
mantra, 11

matter of course, a, 4
meant the world to, 4
merit, 2
miracle, 5
moral high ground, 3
muddled, 2
nagging, 8
narcissism, 1
neurosurgeons, 7
no man's land, 2
notes, 3
nourishment, 1
obsessions, 12
obstacles, 10
opposing arguments, 2
overcome, 1
paralyzed, 11
paraphrase, 7
participation, 9
perfectionist, 8
physician, 8
physicists, 7
ploy, 1
pop culture, 7
potential, 8
poverty, 1
power, 6
prejudices, 10
principles, 11
probability, 10
process (v.), 5
process (n.), 5
proof, 5
prosperity, 1
public health catastrophe, 8
public service, 8
quality of life, 9
quirky, 2
race and class complexities, 12
reflect (on), 11
responsibility, 6
rhyming couplet, 9
ridiculed, 7
rifle, 5
right, 6, 9
sanity, 9
sax, 3
seek solutions, 6
shame, 5
shell-shocked, 4
Shiva call, 4
shot, 2
sit in, 3

stage, 12
stammered out, 4
static, 10
stick to, 4
striving, 8
stumbling blocks, 10
subject (someone) to, 7
superstitious, 1
survival skills, 9
suspected, 1
sustained, 10

sweat the small stuff, 8
sympathy, 4
taking action, 6
tattoo, 7
terrified, 3
tested (one's) faith, 3
textbook space, 12
thirst, 8
torn, 2
transforming, 5
traumatic, 5

trial lawyers, 7
triumph, 5
unequivocal, 4
universe, 3
versus, 4
vibrations, 3
violating, 1
voice (one's) opinion, 6
wager, 3
welder, 3
yearning (for), 2